THE HUMAN SITUATION
A PHILOSOPHICAL ANTHROPOLOGY

The Human Situation

A Philosophical Anthropology

GERD HAEFFNER

Translated by Eric Watkins

UNIVERSITY OF NOTRE DAME PRESS
NOTRE DAME, INDIANA 46556

Originally Published in 1982 as
Philosophische Anthropologie
Copyright © 1982 by Verlag W. Kohlhammer GmbH

Library of Congress Cataloging-in-Publication Data

Haeffner, Gerd.
  [Philosophische Anthropologie. English]
  The human situation : a philosophical anthropology /
Gerd Haeffner; translated by Eric Watkins.
     p.   cm.
  Translation of: Philosophische Anthropologie.
  Bibliography: p.
  Includes index.
  ISBN 0-268-01088-9   — ISBN 0-268-01089-7 (pbk.)
  1. Man.   2. Philosophical anthropology.   I. Title.
BD450.H23613   1989
128—dc19   89-40016

Manufactured in the United States of America

Contents

Introduction

1. Ever since people began to be aware of concerns beyond the necessary fulfillment of fundamental needs, the question has been raised as to the essence, origin, and definition of human beings. Of course, this question has arisen in many different situations, and answers to it have been expressed through various means as well. The question could also remain dormant for periods when people believed that they had sufficient information disposing of the question even before it was raised. Nevertheless the source of the question has never dissipated completely—human beings themselves are too controversial.

2. Even the German and English languages attest to the fact that the human being is a dubious and disquieting creature. Similarly, an ancient experience of this condition is reflected in every language. The etymology is less relevant —as Grimm's dictionary traces the word "human" back to "man—conscious being, (self-)reflection"—than the idiomatic use. In addition to the descriptive use of the word there is also a normative or valuing use. The unusual aspect is that we use the same expressions "man" and "human," depending on the context, to indicate one's high or low status. Expressions of the first kind might be as follows: "an inhumane behavior," "A criminal is still a man." Expressions of the second kind, which most often have the function of being an excuse, would then consist in: "Even a bishop is only a man," or, as Terence might freely be translated, "Nothing human is foreign to me!" "Man" can be an honorable title and an

indication of wretchedness at the same time—can this be a coincidence?

3. What the semantic ambiguity alludes to is widely expressed in the literature of all peoples. Regarding our Western culture one need only refer to two ancient works that can move us even today. The first is the first choral ode from Sophocles' *Antigone,* which begins "Creation is a marvel, and man its masterpiece." The song is filled with wonder about the human being that, in contrast to animals, has no fixed place in the cosmos and, thus, rules all, but is also permeated with fear because human beings cannot always be integrated into the artificial home of urban society. The second text is Psalm 8, which expresses the awareness that humans are minute and transient compared with the eternally moving stars in the heavens and culminates in the question, directed to the Creator, "What is man that you think of him, mere man, that you care for him?" The gamut of human behavior, ability, and existence extends to both extremes.

4. To a certain extent we can still understand today the ancient accounts of wonder and pondering about human beings. However, in current times the lack of insight concerning human beings has taken on a new acuteness. To begin with, one could mention the collapse of the traditional relationship to nature. Formerly nature was experienced as something to be contained, but still being overwhelming and inexhaustible, an entity which one could exploit all the more as long as one was sure of its indestructibility, or, in a sense, its maternal dependability. Today we perceive nature as a scarce reserve (also as regards Romantic naturalness), for which we thoughtfully plan and must care for well. Nature as a limitation for human beings has disappeared in favor of exploitable and enjoyable surroundings to be protected. In a relatively short period of time the scientific industrial revolution, the reason for this change, dissolved certain outdated modes of coexistence and, therefore, a certain orientation to life. At the same time it freed completely new

and very extensive possible courses of action whose ethical and humane value is increasingly being discussed. This discussion will, without fail, reach the roots of values and convictions handed down by tradition.

Regardless of these new questions, our self-understanding received a heavy blow when confronted with the atrocities of genocide and of the past world wars. How were such things possible in such a progressive Western civilization in the twentieth century? What tendencies must be in human beings that enabled such things to happen? The mass of (often contradictory) attempts at explanation could only fall back on a solid religious, humanitarian, and scientific foundation. In such a manner human beings that at least stem from Western culture experienced themselves more and more as beings that did not know what they were, for what reason they were there, and how they should live.

5. Due to this awareness the question as to the nature of human beings has increasingly come to the forefront in philosophy, a question which had existed under the title "anthropology" since its inception. A similar movement took place in the realm of the sciences as new ways and directions in which to study human beings emerged and developed. In this process there is a lively discussion between the various scientific and philosophical thematizations of humanity, mediated by the simple commonsense wisdom from which both projects grow. However, philosophical anthropology is not merely referenced to empirical research; it is also dependent on other philosophical disciplines, perhaps even more than they are dependent upon it. For what the nature of knowledge, moral obligation, and such is is not cleared up by referring back to previously gained (from where?) anthropological knowledge. On the contrary, knowledge of human beings consists in the results that stem from epistemology (theory of knowledge), metaphysics, the foundations of ethics, and so on, albeit always under the special perspective of acts in human existence and the unity of these acts, not the objective validity of propositions. The proper

optics that allow for such a synthetic question can only be ontological, concerned with being, reality, at its most profound level, but they can only be worked out in the analysis of partial and preontological realistic features.
6. Philosophical anthropology stands for the path of knowledge concerned with the nature or essence of human beings: the typical form of existence, the inner structure and dynamics, and other concerns. The use of this title does not indicate any adherence to the school of thought that has placed itself or was placed under that name: that philosophical direction whose most important proponents were M. Scheler (1961), H. Plessner (1928), and A. Gehlen (1988) and whose most important thesis was that the question as to the nature of human beings, primarily raised in reference to biological research, is the central question of philosophy.
7. Philosophical anthropology is of course to be distinguished from anthropology, which is concerned with certain directions of empirical research: physical anthropology and cultural anthropology (ethnology)—a field with varying, yet interwoven, investigations (see Schwitdetzky 1975)—which does not have anything more than its name in common with philosophical anthropology.
8. The anthropological question in this book is worked out in the form of an analysis of analysis through different levels of questioning whereby the transition from one level to the next should proceed from the awareness that the motivating question has been shown to be insufficiently answered on the basis of the results of a certain level of questioning. Thus, our question will initially be asked with an outlook stemming from natural science. The difficulties of this approach point to the necessity, on the one hand, of introducing an ontological framework and, on the other hand, of incorporating scientific-pragmatic reflection into the considerations (Part A). Both of these moments converge in the idea of a worldly subjectivity that is to be a principle of organization for the whole delineation. This idea receives an initial illustration in the interpretation of several basic dimensions

of human being-in-the-world which is carried out with recourse to theory models of selected humanity sciences (Part B). An analysis of those basic modes of human subjectivity that can be indicated by the terms "consciousness" and "freedom of choice" leads further into the center of the issue (Part C). Finally, the question concentrates on the search for the fundamental unity and for the realizable meaning of the human condition (Part D).

9. Because each human being is, according to one old metaphor, a world in himself (a microcosm), such a short portrayal naturally cannot be more than a kind of introduction to the outline of anthropological questions. As such it does not attempt to contribute to research, although it does contain the hope that some readers will be able to recognize their own questions within, find stimulation for further questioning, and perhaps obtain some knowledge. Because the structure of the whole book could have been reversed and because every philosophical text has its beginning from the end, moving backward, it shall be necessary to read through the text at least twice. Much is intentionally only hinted at in order not to rob the reader of having his or her own joy of discovery. Illustration of the text with historical references has been omitted almost completely as the limited space does not allow for either a just portrayal or criticism of positions, and the issue-oriented presentation of the topics considered is to have definite priority.

A. The Question as to the Correct Approach

10. The situation from which our question proceeds is ignorance, the lack of explicit and justified knowledge. How are we supposed to arrive at such knowledge? The first and most natural place to turn is to the sciences, or, to be more precise, the rigorous form of natural science. The reason for this is not merely that this procedure is suggested by the basic outlook of our modern culture. It would simply be presumptuous to pass by what a large number of researchers have already achieved before us in their laborious work of investigations, analyses, and discussions of these analyses.

I. The Approach from Comparative Biology

11. If we order the natural sciences according to their degree of generality, we find that biology is the first science in which "human being" occurs. "Human beings" do not arise in physics or chemistry as an object of study. Of course human beings do fall under the realm of these sciences insofar as they are bodies in space or a complex of chemical bonds and processes, but not in a manner that differs specifically from other bodies, processes, and so on. The object of study for biology, however, is an ordered field of living organisms. In the systematic and evolutionary whole of living organisms there are differing places in which the name "man" (homo sapiens) occurs. (To ask to what extent the results of biological research can be formulated, in a second step, within the current theories of chemistry and physics is a different question. That is, whether the ontological irreducibility of living organisms to inorganic matter corresponds to the methodological independence of biology as opposed to the putatively more basic sciences of physics and chemistry. We shall address this problem, which belongs to the realm of philosophy of nature, in later places to the extent that it is required by our anthropological aims. See No. 137–141, 165 f., 210–216.)

12. The method a biologist uses to make statements about human beings is one of comparing individuals of one species with individuals of other similar and ancestrally related

9

species. Such a comparison is always directed in a particular way. If one expects very basic differences, one will be surprised by the extensive similarities. This can lead to the impression that there are hardly any differences at all. (This is often the effect, if not also the purpose, of reports in the simplified popularization of science.) However, if one assumes the similarities as a basis, the special differences come forth expressly, but not exaggeratedly (see Portmann, 1974, 100–104).

The first determination of what human beings are resides in the place that they have within the system of living organisms. A look at the table representing the natural system of living organisms shows that we are dealing with a mammal (not an amphibian), with a primate (not a rodent), with an anthropoid and not a member of a different primate group. Again, there is a further relationship between human beings and baboons than with chimpanzees, gorillas, and orangutans. This placement of the human being, not the fruition of a quick look, but rather of methodological investigations, enables one to note and interpret further special aspects by way of comparison and analogy. We shall see that the extent to which human beings differ from their biological relatives greatly exceeds the normal degree of differences between related species (especially between the different groups of the anthropoid apes).

The most important peculiarities of human beings, as far as they are observable by biologists, can be summarized according to three aspects: anatomical-morphological, ontogenetical, and ethological.

1. ANATOMICAL-MORPHOLOGICAL PECULIARITIES

13. In comparison to the anthropoid ape the skeleton of the human being is decisively altered: S-shaped curvature of the spine beginning on the lower side of the skull; the pelvis is less erect; the hip and knee joints are almost completely

extended (in an erect position); the feet are arched; and so on. All of these qualities correspond to the erect posture that the human being—the only mammal with this quality—has constantly. The correlates of this erect posture are the liberation of the front extremities from ambulatory tasks and the development of the capability of a standing foot, whereas the chimpanzee has four hands, so to speak, and walks on the outsides of its "feet." In accordance with their life, mainly in the trees, the hand of anthropoids (as contrasted with human beings) is a lengthened "hook-hand" with a relatively small thumb that does not, to any great extent, stand in opposition to the hand. The hand of the human being is much less specialized and, due to its liberation from transportation tasks, more differentiated in that it is appropriate not only for a powerful grip but also for precise and delicate work.

14. The free use of the hand—the "tool of tools" (Aristotle, *De anima* III, 8)—has a close connection with the form of the skull. The eyes, positioned more to the front, viewing stereoscopically, and the corresponding receding muzzlelike protrusion of the face are emphasized in the case of the human being. This implies a dominance of the visual and tactile senses over the olfactory sense (see Plessner 1970: "Anthropologie der Sinne"). The defensive eyeteeth have become less developed, as have the overly strong muscles in the jaw area—compensation for the new capacity of the hands to transport objects and to carry tools and weapons. This development enables the complex of organs involved in sound production to change in such a manner that a more differentiated production of sounds becomes possible as is necessary for human languages. The forehead that does not need to provide a basis for strong chewing muscles is "unlocked"; the cranium can become larger and offer more space for the brain.

15. The brain, being the most important part of the central nervous system, plays a decisive role for the organization of more developed living organisms, a role which in-

creases in the process of evolution. The human being does not have more parts in the brain. However, the volume of its brain is greater than that of other anthropoids: a human brain being 1300 cm³ as opposed to that of a gorilla as approximately 500 cm³. What is even clearer is the comparison of the relative brain weights (as compared to body weight). In addition to the more developed size, the differentiation within the brain (different parts having different distributions) plays a decisive role: a human being's phylogenetically older cerebellum which is responsible for the realms of affective and instinctive reactions is noticeably atrophied, whereas the relatively new cerebrum (cortex) that allows for higher functions is extraordinarily well developed. The high density of neuron connection is especially noticeable. At this point a few key factors must suffice.

2. ONTOGENETICALLY EXCEPTIONAL STANDPOINT

16. Perhaps the most important event in one's life is one's birth, taking one from the protected and cared for life in the mother's womb to an existence as an abandoned being. All of the higher forms of mammals have gestation periods whose length is determined by their degree of development. According to this "law" human beings ought to have a gestation period of 21 to 22 months, although it is in fact, as everyone knows, only 9 months. Another observation points in the same direction. For almost all animals the end of the gestation period coincides with the completion of the maturation of capacities that are necessary for a self-sufficient life; the rate of maturation that continues then declines relatively quickly thereafter. The maturation of the neuromuscular organization of the small human being, however, continues for about a year at approximately the same rate as before. For this reason Portmann called the first year of a human being's life the "extrauterine year of the embryo." The impor-

tance of this anomaly is that in this manner the cultural-social formation of the infant reaches (and correspondingly deeply) into the stage of its embryonic immaturity. "In the time from the ninth to the eleventh month of the first year . . . three important features of human existence are formed simultaneously: the use of tools, language, and the erect posture" (Portmann 1942, 21). "In all of these endeavors hereditary predispositions, and the desire to imitate the surroundings act in intimately connected ways. A similar situation is not possible for any of the other higher forms of mammals—they experience all of these decisive graphic phases of their neuromuscular organization in the mother's womb in which a fixed organization of instincts can be implanted far from all contact with the outside world" (ibid. 20).

3. PECULIARITIES OF THE STRUCTURE OF BEHAVIOR

17. The behavior of animals in certain situations is either completely, or for the most part, determined by the kind of species to which it belongs and independently of the experiences it has had. Moreover, their behavior is directed toward advancing the individual, its group, and its genetic potential. "In numerous cases an organism reacts to a certain biologically important (outer) stimulus without any previous experience, without trial and error, immediately and in a determinate way that is sensibly directed toward the survival of the species" (Lorenz 1943, 249). The assignment of certain configurations of sense data to certain kinds of reactions allows for an optimum chance of acting "correctly" in any situation. Changes in the surroundings and in the organisms in these surroundings are represented to the animal by schemata that effectively induce the corresponding reactions when the (hormone-guided) inner disposition is there. The partial reactions in this process are integrated into a

meaningful series of actions that lead to a provisional goal (satisfaction of hunger, copulation, clarification of social order, etc.); every one of these partial reactions is brought about by a new stimulus. Thus, there is a hierarchy: from the encompassing end of the survival of the individual and species through the satisfaction of basic needs (satisfaction of hunger, reproduction, etc.) to the attainment of partial goals (e.g., for reproduction: the elimination of rivals) and from there to the specific actions (here, e.g., in battle: track, threaten, bite, etc.). What is important is that the animal does not have to learn which behavior is appropriate in any given situation, but rather already "knows," that is, proceeds as if it had known it all along. This does not exclude the behavior of animals being determined by other factors that are not innate; this is especially true for higher vertebrates. In such cases, on the one hand, there is imprinting; on the other hand, learning. One speaks of imprinting "when in a certain sensitive phase (of life) sense impressions have the effect of inextricably becoming the effective stimulus for future reactions in a certain operational area" (Hassenstein 1972, 61). One can explain, for example, the stability of the mother-child relationship and the determination of one's sexual orientation (one's "type" of partner) through imprinting. New modes of reaction can be attained if they grow out of the innate instincts through repeated sensations of pain or pleasure. The more developed an animal species is, the more capable it will be to gain experience through trial and error and to change its behavior through learning (i.e., the simple adoption of other's behavior). The stubbornness of one's "instinctual equipment" remains, although it may be complemented by the reservoir of imprintings and learned behavior.

18. For the human being the balance of elements that determine behavior is more on the side of tradition and insight. Thus, the whole framework of behavior determinants is altered.

The automatic connection of stimulus and response can

be inhibited by thought processes as opposed to the driving function of the stimulus.

The various dispositions to act ("instincts") along with their corresponding objects are not clearly distinguishable anymore but rather are transformable to a great extent. To a point one can separate the drives for nutrition, reproduction, and acceptance. "However, in the what and how of their objectives, expression, and exclusivity (they are) unpredictable" (Gehlen 1961, 114). Accordingly, anorexia and binging can have sexual causes just as different sexual behavior patterns are sometimes only comprehensible as an expression of the desire for power and acceptance. Tied in with this aspect is the fact that the tendency toward sexual activity for human beings is much less rhythmical (i.e., in seasons of heat) than in related animals. The permanence of sexual responsiveness, however, leads "to a continuous, lasting sexualization of all human motivational systems on the one hand—but also to an important permeation of sexual activities with the continuously effective other motives of human behavior" (Portmann 1956, 63f.).

19. The most important and central difference is a radical novelty on the side of motives as well as on the corresponding side of objects: the human being is capable not only of receiving objects as complexes of stimuli but also of interpreting and respecting them as independent existing beings—up to the point of creating a system of ethics and critical ontology. The capability and the motive for such behavior refer to an end that stands above the end of survival and reproduction. For this reason human beings can relinquish reproduction for other goals; they themselves can give their lives an aim or risk their lives for an important cause.

II. The Difficulty of This Approach

This cursory discussion of the three selected biological approaches to the nature of human beings exemplifies a difference that exceeds the normal degree of difference between animals of the same genus. It goes so far as to make the similarities between a horse and a gorilla, observed with the whole mode of life in view, appear larger than those between a gorilla and a human. A difference between humanity and animality, as such, suggests itself. How is it conceivable that a special animal species—human beings—is distinguished from animals?

20. One can attempt to sidestep the paradox by interpreting the peculiarity of human beings merely as a part of their attempt at satisfying basic needs and attaining goals of survival and reproduction just as animals do. This conception views the human being, along with A. Gehlen, for example, as a "faulty being" that attempts to compensate as well as possible for a lack of hair through clothing, a lack of weaponry in the form of teeth and claws through clubs and atomic bombs, and a lack of instinctual provisions through social institutions. Of course, these faults occur only through reference to an ideal picture of an animal and not a specifically human norm. The human being appears faulty only when one takes the animal's attainment of survival and reproduction of its species as the standard. Whether this standard is the correct standard for human beings, that is, is of its essence, is really the question. The question is not at all

answered simply by referring to the far-reaching analogy between human beings and other hominoids. For the foundation of a definition of the essence of a certain being is not constituted by abstract, identical features but rather their integration into a complete character. The reference to the common origin of humanoids and human beings out of the same phylum would only guarantee an essential identity of both life forms if it were already clear that nothing really new could come into existence during the course of evolution. Accordingly, one is forced to agree with W. Schulz's judgment (1972, 443): "The motive of survival functions for Gehlen as an abstract principle from which and toward which interpretation unfolds. In short: Gehlen assumes a biological metaphysics."

21. Another solution to the paradox that the human being is an animal and at the same time different from animals as such can be provided by a dualism which views human beings as composed of two components: that of a desiring body, which is shared with animals, and that of spirit, which is unique. M. Scheler presented an especially strong form of dualism in his late programmatic work *Man's Place in Nature*. In it he claims that the originality of human beings is the ability to say No to desires. Scheler transfers the unity of desires and spirit which must be prior to their conflict back into a (tragically divided) divinity, that is, an absolute being. The problem for dualism lies in grasping the unity of human being. Moreover, dualism often overlooks the fact that the human body is something quite different from an animal's: in the special form in which the human "soul" finds congenial expression as well as in the special way of having a body. The human being is not half-animal and half-angel but rather a complete human being.

22. In order to see this wholeness, we must abandon the biological viewpoint, while taking its rich yield with us. For this viewpoint is neither the sole nor the basic way in which we can form an idea of our essence. From the phenomenal side the numerous sciences of human beings or of humanity

are to be at least partially taken into consideration: ethnology, psychology, medicine, sociology, religious studies, music, and so on: sciences that study the forms of and reasons for human actions, interpersonal interaction, and production as well as the inner structure of typical human products (and in the light of their producers). If we stick to these sciences, we do this with the awareness that they build on something that is indispensable for their interpretation: everyday experience. On the conceptual side, however, a level must be found that enables one to escape the dilemma posed above. This quandary arose because human beings and anthropoids alike (and other animals) were conceived of under a general concept of animal that was formed for nonhuman animals so that either biological reductionism or dualism remained as solutions for the determination of human beings.

23. Aside from the difficulties of these attempts at a solution of the paradox, we should note that one cannot succeed in finding a concept of animal in whose definition human beings are not at least secretly demarcated. We interpret the behavior and makeup of animals with anthropomorphic expressions, even when we try to keep the anthropomorphism within reasonable limits. Conversely, we interpret our own behavior in light of the interpreted behavior of animals. In this manner our understanding of animals and humans grows, while not yet on a theoretical or thematic foundation. Understanding of both is gained simultaneously, yet by contrast with one another (see Buytendijk 1958, 8.120–124). This does not criticize behavior research, comparative anatomy, and so on, rather only the philosophical ambition of making biology the basis of philosophical anthropology.

24. The level of theory on which the question as to the nature of human beings can adequately be treated is the ontological level. Only on this level can the three requirements raised by the nature of the question be satisfied:

a) The general concept that encompasses the various modes of animality as well as the unique meaning structure of human beings is so general that it can only be formed by ontological concepts. The matter concerns a concept for which the English language does not possess an adequate word as compared with Greek in which the expression "zoon" contains "animal," "human," and even "divine" life, whereas the English living (animate) being contains the realm of plants as such, and the spiritual life only in metaphorical extension. For this reason we shall choose the technical term "subject" as the expression of the concept to be introduced shortly, as it has been by other authors as well.

b) The question as to the essence of something refers to the circumscription or basic structure of the existence of something. Within this question we are looking for a method in which something must be interpreted for its ultimate and most comprehensive idea of being, beyond a mere list of the different modes of appearance and beyond an understanding that remains oriented toward the idea of functionality. The form of the question as to the nature of something is ontological (see M. Müller 1974, 11–20). This does not mean that the question as to the nature of human beings can be answered simply by recurring to a previously prepared ontology. Rather, ontology and anthropology are formed in constant reciprocity (see Haeffner 1980).

c) The sought-after concept of the nature of human beings must not only render comprehensible all components that are shown in the everyday, commonsensical, or scientific phenomenon "human being" but also account for the fact of research, interpretation, and comprehension itself. As we shall see, this will carry us from the level of real presence (inanimate objects) to the level of living comprehension that is reflected in ontological categories.

III. The Concept of the Subject

The matter at hand is (1) to introduce a concept of the subject as a certain act of unity by starting with the ontological categories of "being" and "one" and then (2) to explain the concept in its correlation to the idea of the world.

1. SUBJECTIVITY AS THE FORM OF UNITY

25. The ideas of being (true reality) and unity can take the place of one another: wherever we find being, we also find unity, and vice versa. The less something appears real to us, the less real unity it has.

When one speaks of a unit, one thinks of the elements of counting: $1 + 1 + 1 + \ldots$. The presupposition of being counted is that the units have something in common which enables them to be taken together—and that every element has an inner compactness and delineation from others through which it can be taken as one at all, regardless of whether it is also placed in a sequence with others. This unity becomes more obvious when one considers a possible change in the sameness (identity) of what is changing or the possibility of dissecting a whole into its parts. If one analyzes different beings—a stone found anywhere, a household utensil, a dog, a human being—in light of the idea of unity, an increased intensity of realized unity is manifest—an increase that is parallel to the well-known series in the order of be-

20

ing. Via this exemplary application the concept of subjectivity (now to be presented as a result), understood as an act of unity, receives the contour of its meaning and the test of its productivity. We shall begin with unity (inner compactness and delineation from others) as it presents itself to an observer, and then proceed to the difference-unity of one's self and others, as it is actualized by the particular subject itself.

a) Steps of Objective Sameness and Wholeness

26. I have "a" stone in my hand. On what does its unity rest? The consistency of the material hardly plays a role. What is more important is the compactness of its form (that one can move from any point of its surface to another such that the movement will eventually repeat itself), and that this form lasts at least for a few moments or longer. A regular geometrical form makes our judgment easier when we ask ourselves after a stone has been broken into two pieces whether we have two pieces of one stone or two stones in front of us. In a similar vein, we divide a train of mountains into different "individual" mountains. Measurement plays a greater or lesser role—at any rate it cannot completely be excluded in favor of pure objectivity. For through measurement the pattern of commodities is very important for the interpretation of an object.

A commodity (like a knife or a ball) has a clear unity that it owes to the demarcation of its purpose and toward which its production was directed. The concept of purpose allows for knowing that the individual parts fit into a whole. Accordingly, we judge which changes threaten the identity of an object and which are superficial. Similarly, for this reason we see certain states of a whole as faulty or deranged. Therefore, the concept of purpose functions as the principle of the unity of an object. This idea stands the test when one proceeds to interpret living organisms. In such cases the organism has, in contrast with the commodity, a purpose (meaning) in itself (in its "double life" as an individual and as a species)—although not independent of its place and function in the whole of nature. If, however, the organism were to be exhausted by its function, then the whole, to which each organism is relative, would have no meaning. For the whole only has its existence in the individual organisms. Thus, the living organism carries in itself a principle of identity that is retained and acquired through metamorphosis, metabolism, development, and other changes. It also has a principle of identity in and through itself—and not merely such that every judgment about faulty parts has its standard in the natural structure of the being itself, but also such that this standard is the dynamic origin for the development of the parts that belong to the whole (organs, functions, etc.) or for their regeneration and reciprocal compensation.

b) Steps of the Subjective Act of Unity

27. Now we have proceeded from the unity of the object of knowledge to the unity of the being itself. Seen from the perspective of the more or less clear unity of an object of knowledge, a stone sphere, a telephone booth, a cow, and a human being are on the same level. However, this is not the case for the being's own inner unity. Due to the original and dynamic character that is peculiar to a living organism's principle of unity, its unity is greater than that of a commodity. For the same reason the unity of a dog is greater than that of a lilac bush, just as that of a human being is greater than that of a gorilla. For this dynamics claims a difference not only between the parts and the whole that precedes these parts—that is, not only between a living organism and its various states—but rather also between the living organism and *its* counterpart.

28. It belongs to the unity of a stone that it is not at the same time something else. This property of not being something else belongs to its this-ness, but both sameness (identity) and not other-ness (not difference) are nothing for the

stone itself but rather only for the observer. For the stone there is neither itself nor anything else because it does not possess the structural capacity of "for . . .": that existential reflexivity that distinguishes an organism to the degree that it is organized. For the same reason one cannot apply the concepts of activity and passivity to a stone. Granted, in such cases there are passive and active relations in a grammatical sense: "The stone is being warmed by the sun"; "The stone is pressing on the ground." However, due to the fact that this pressing does not proceed from any real spontaneity, it stands on the same level as being warmed does: prior to the presence of the difference of activity and passivity (which is constitutive for both). This is very different for living organisms, especially for animals! For they have achieved a basic presence in which it itself as well as other things (in states of feeling: comfort, pain, restlessness, etc. and in perception) can be *for it*. This presence is involved in the dynamics of desires for the development and survival of the individual species' existence that directs an animal to possible prey, sexual partners, offspring, companions, foes, foxholes, and so on. This directing to others is "preprogrammed" not only into its structure of behavior but also into its entire organization (sense, propulsion, digestive and reproductive organs, etc.). Both sides develop evolutionarily and ontogenetically as correlates. Thus, the other thing belongs, in its diversity, to the animal, and not merely conceptually but also in its real and constitutive reciprocity. For this reason activity and passivity clearly diverge; an animal reacts differently to a physiological stimulus when the stimulus is actively expected than when it meets the animal by surprise. (See von Buytendijk 1958, 43, for instructive examples of a jellyfish which meets with a stick: in the first case it feels around the object; in the second it pulls back from the stick.)

29. Let us supplement this overly brief sketch with a look at the circumstances for human beings! Here we find an increase in all aspects of unity (which is not to be confused with harmony, although it is a condition of the possibility

for an otherwise impossible division as well as for an otherwise inconceivable harmony).

The individual unity is extensively increased. A human being exceeds the framework of significance and function for the species and the entirety of nature to a degree which no other animal does. The significance accorded by the species recedes behind the meaning that lies in the "truly human" structure of life attainable individually and socially; a human being can take on so many roles, relations, and functions and still remain the same, so that this multiplicity must be grounded in a very autonomous and central principle of identity. This implies that the task of integration, of each new acquisition of wholeness, increases immensely. For the horizon of human beings extends far beyond the survival and reproduction of biological life; it is the idea of a meaningful life. Each person, within her horizon, must integrate everything that she encounters into the synthesis of a single world via repeated methods. Whatever she encounters, she encounters such that the other being (especially another person) can bring its own life along—such that the other can be "there" in its own existence and worth. To the human mode of existence belongs the knowledge which refers, in the horizon of truth, to what *is,* and the free choice that determines, in the horizon of the idea of the good, what should be the case —as shall be presented in detail in the chapter on the conscious side of human beings. Life within the horizons mentioned is a basic act of unity, in principle and in each concrete case. Thus, "the soul is in a sense all existing things" (Aristotle, *De anima* III, 8 431b 21).

Out of this basic unity with everything arises consciousness as a self existing in opposition to others. For—as shall be shown below—the actual known and the actual knowing are identical—and in such a way that the awareness of the difference between the knower in itself and the known in itself lives in this identity. The same is true for the acts of striving and loving. Knowing and loving are acts of an identity whose emphasis is placed contraposed: in knowledge in the knower (as that which "has" known something); in love in the loved one (i.e., in the existence that is affirmed). Knowledge is being-at-another in the form of being-at-oneself; love is being-at-oneself in the form of being-at-another.

30. We shall call a "subject" a being that has its being in the act of a relational unity in which it and other(s) stand out for the subject as separate units. In short, a "subject" is a being that is related to itself in that it is related to others.

We have now found the—analogous—general concept which enables a comparison of human beings and animals. We can also already see that this concept is sufficient for the other demands that were made in No. 24. To what extent this concept can be applied—whether it can be extended so far as to cover lower animals and plants—is a question that belongs to the philosophy of nature. The anthropologist can be content that this concept provides the main idea for the analysis, while at the same time preparing a basis for the formulation of the undeniable relatedness of, as well as the just as undeniable difference between, human beings and animals.

31. Since the word "subject" is ambiguous, one must understand that the meaning intended here is that of a real being with a determinate mode of existence and not the grammatical subject of a sentence. "Subjectivity" means this mode of existence and has nothing to do with "subjective" in the sense of coincidental, nonobjective ("merely subjective"). In relation to the use of the word according to which subjectivity is intended only when the carrier of mental acts is concerned, we shall use the word here in a broader sense to include human unconscious and (at any rate higher) animal life. We cannot go into the origin of this ambiguous word from the perspective of the history of ontology.

2. SUBJECTIVITY AS BEING-IN-THE-WORLD

32. "The animal and human organism form a relationship to their surroundings that is not only the condition for

the intraorganic processes of life but also exists *with* the animal or human being *for* and *through it* as a significant system. This coliving, lived, and structured surrounding is called the surroundings of the animal and the world of human beings" (Buytendijk 1958, 18). Subjectivity and world belong together. Having a world distinguishes a subject (which is a "substance" in the fullest sense) from a mere object. Subject and others (counterparts) are correlative. A thing is what it is; a subject is how and to what it is related. The "how" and goal of behavior do not arise completely new and isolated but rather stand in a certain connection to their manifold. Each individual event, each single mode of action, receives its meaning from a larger structured context, either completely or partially. This context is the "world" of the particular subject: from the perspective of the whole (the world of human beings; the world of foxes, etc.) or from the perspective of certain realms of life (the world of the youth/elderly; the world of the pariah/the officer; the world of mathematics, work, fashion, etc.).

33. "World" in this sense is an anthropological concept that must be distinguished from the cosmological concept of world. Formally, "world" refers to a totality. In the cosmological concept of world we grasp the totality of all real things, seen in themselves, that interact with each other (without interaction there would be several separate worlds). The anthropological concept of world has as a distinguishing feature the possessive case: it is the world *of* the Frenchman, the world *of* the man, and so on: the totality of meaningful objects for a subject. Thus, it is clear that these concepts of world are formally different. The anthropological "world" is not just a section of the cosmological world, although it is true that only a small part of the world of real things as they are in themselves can be present or represented in the world of each subject. For the subjective world is not the totality of beings, perceived by an observer as such, that are present in the spatial neighborhood of a subject (in its spatial manifestation). A world is relative to certain acts of a

subject that render possible this world, because the range of possibly meaningful objects is prescribed and demarcated through them. For the world of the rich, for example, the same amount of money plays a completely different role than it does for the world of the poor; a human being who grew up in the country experiences nature differently than one who grew up in the city. Everything has a somewhat different meaning for such a human being, and she will act correspondingly in nature. However, the world of a human being is very malleable. The world can be developed further (in the process of learning) as well as extended or solidified.

34. Strictly speaking, the world in which one lives is never the same as the world in which one lived before; the world of one organism is never the world of another. However, the world of human beings has features from its structure in its ontogeny and socialization that are common to all, many, or, at least, several human beings, although everyone lives in their own world, as seen from a broad perspective. These common features are found in the worlds of human beings and to a greater extent in the worlds of those animals for whom individuality is less marked than for human beings. In addition, to a certain degree human beings have the capability of understanding another human being or even an animal in its world — or in other words, of projecting oneself into the world of another, whether it be by living together or in an attempt at understanding each other. This passing over the borders of one's own world into the center of another world is a difficult endeavor and is quickly confronted with the rigid walls of foreignness. Nevertheless, that the human being has empathy to a minimal extent (putting oneself in the place of another) and can strive for a greater degree of empathy, and that a human being can suffer due to its inner limits when they cannot be extended, constitute the structure of all human worlds. In this sense one speaks of the world of human beings as open in contrast to the closed world of animals whose borders can only be varied somewhat and, at any rate, exclude in principle

all forms of border transgression (in the knowledge of limitedness).

Heidegger's *Being and Time* provides an example of a human world that remains informative even today, namely, a phenomenological interpretation of the world of a craftsman. Heidegger attempts in this work to characterize the world that, in both an ongoing and limiting sense, lies prior to the project of producing, for example, a shoe which is centrally positioned for the use of the hammer: a specific presence of materials, techniques, aids, customers, coworkers, one's own capacities (or lack thereof), and so on, all for the craftsman himself who lives completely for the product. This world is "hung up," in a sense, on the product that is anticipated in the plans and realized in the work. It remains modifiable: not only because the shoemaker can be retrained into a bus driver but also because the world that gives him security can decay from within in the face of the experience of the transience or even meaninglessness of life. While living in the everyday world in which we are always concerned about attaining some intermediate goal and are, thus, living "inauthentically," the world is open and cannot be essentially closed. This shows at the same time the limits of the possibilities of an "authentic" mode of existence that consists in the personal acceptance of one's own finitude. The being-in-the-world is not left behind in it but rather accepted on its own.

35. The relatively closed, everyday world that is oriented toward production deteriorated into the "they" and, outwardly directed, is not to be placed on the same level as the closed world of an animal. The experiment with crickets which Uexküll (1956, 62) reports in his stimulating, although in many points now outdated, book *Excursions through the Environments of Animals and People* shows clearly that a cricket male does not perceive the acoustic and optic stimuli of a cricket female as being expressions of one and the same being. The stimuli remain bound by the preprogrammed mating process such that they are only perceived if they oc-

cur at a specific time within the whole process to whose
unity—not the unity of the carrier of expressions—they refer. Thus such a cricket male would have no world that extends beyond the here and now of the stimuli situation. For
the configuration of the stimulus-response chain is a pattern, but only for the eye of the researcher and not for the
cricket. Nevertheless, it would seem as if one could still speak
of a kind of world and, thus, of subjectivity in a relatively
responsible sense of the word with a view to the mode of
existence of *higher* forms of animal life. Of course, the application of concepts onto animals, obtained from an interpretation of human relations, is always a difficult issue, and
an analogous way of speaking would have to be justified in
each specific case. Everyday talk about animals tends to use
anthropomorphisms, whereas scientific discourse leans toward mechanisms. While we are acquainted with the human
and machines are comprehensible for us, we can only understand animals through convergence from both sides. In principle they remain foreign to us, and all the more so the more
we develop away from being similar to them.

IV. The Problem of the Unity of the Sought-After Concept of Human Existence

We are searching for a definition of the essence of human beings. However, do the various different human beings even have a common essence that can be captured in a concept? Even if this may be assumed, can this essence be captured by human beings, whose thought is rooted in a certain culture, a certain history, and so on? We shall have to consider briefly both of these methodological problems.

1. UNITY OF THE ESSENCE

36. The definition of an essence should be applicable to all of the members of a class of objects and only these members. Moreover, such a definition should provide one with the basic existential structure that can be attributed to these beings in essentially the same way (not just analogously). The form is the same as in all definitions. The identity of a concept can clearly be transcribed if a definition is indebted to the existence of this concept before problems regarding its application to the phenomena are considered. The identity of mathematical concepts that express the structure of abstract entities are of such a nature. The identity of the content of empirical concepts, conversely, is something which must prove itself through its manifold realizations. If it is to be, not an arbitrarily and abstractly constructed concept,

but rather the concept of an essence, the power of the essence must be exhibited throughout its realizations. The necessity that every single living organism must die in order to make room for other living organisms which it has produced (out of a natural desire and capability) displays a certain command of the natural kind over the single beings, an identity in difference, a constant in coming to be and passing away. The individual natural kinds of living organisms can be distinguished by the criterion of sexual fertility. "A human being begets a human being" is the formulation Aristotle has already expressed. The argument remains valid despite being restricted in its application. The decisive limitation is not that we — since the discovery of the equality of female and male reproductive cells — must say today, "Two human beings bring forth a human being," but rather that we must augment the old question, whether an infant can be called a human being in the same sense as an adult, with the new question as to the phylogenetic and transcultural identity of human beings. Adults and infants are in continuous development. If one moves away from the phenotype to the genotype, the identity of the essence will be easy to determine. Still, the basic features of human beings can primarily be read off an adult. For example, it is true for an adult and not for an infant that it possesses linguistic skills. On the level of one's capabilities in principle (not actuality) the identity appears again. The grown-up as well as the newly born human being is a being that has in principle linguistic and comprehension capabilities.

37. This solution sketches a way out of the other difficulties that arose from the phylogenetic and cultural variety. Humanity reaches as far back phylogenetically as (in the recourse from present human beings to their ancestors) distinct differences remain from related anthropoids that reveal an inner continuity toward those differences in morphological, behavioral, and other aspects that stand today as a sign of essential differences between human beings and anthropoids. We read the typical human qualities — such as lan-

guage, technology, and abstract thought—off of the present, formalize these concepts until the earliest manifestations can still be subsumed under them, and then affirm as a partial definition of the essence of human beings a capacity that underlies all of these manifestations. However, since one would say that today's technology and linguistic culture express to a greater extent (taken as a whole) what technology and language can be than did the production of rock machines and (probably) the corresponding mode of communication 2 million years ago, one would also have to say that human beings have become realized to an increasing extent during the course of history. The actual expressions corresponding to one's essence would, thus, be in an analogous unity within themselves (thus, not used unequivocally), whereas the essence of the different human beings that gives rise to the merely analogous expression of itself would remain constant.

This claim can be attacked from two sides: the one set of antagonists would say that there is no unity in the essence but rather merely an analogy of appearances, that the definition of the essence must be discarded. The other group would disavow taking today's human beings as the high point on the graduated scale and claim, instead, that there is an equality of all manifestations since they are manifestations of precisely one kind of being.

38. The first of the antitheses can take for granted that the transition from mere animality to humanity is so unnoticeable that it seems to be a matter of more or less arbitrary classification as to when human beings began to exist. Thus, it seems tempting to refrain from affirming any essential difference at all and to be content with registering certain phenomenal kinds of differences that increase throughout the course of time. One is, however, then forced to understand the difference that exists today between the orangutans and human beings not as one between different essences. This position has, at the same time, the consequences that the essential differences in the behavior of human beings and

orangutans cannot be interpreted in a natural way and that differences in duties between orangutans and human beings (which can only be based in the essence) do not exist; these are consequences which the limitation to the merely empirical level of concept formation reveals to be a withdrawal from the realm of comprehension and practical morality. Conversely, it becomes obvious that the definition of an essence can never be reduced to a permeation of the phenomena alone but rather that it must take evidence from the moral realm into consideration. (That there is evidence for an objective morality and that concrete moral duties are not merely formal, but rather can only be grounded by the being to whom they are binding, must be shown in ethics.) Of course, it is difficult and in the end impossible to give a precise point at which a creature is transformed from being a "mere" animal into a human being, but why should it not be the case that something essentially new could have developed, necessarily almost unnoticeably, out of its previous stages? The nonderivability of novelty that entered into the world along with the human being is much greater than the nonderivability of the manifold of living organisms from the prehistoric forms of material. However, if the latter is accepted, one is more prepared to accept the former.

39. The second antithesis starts with the prejudice that every activity of a being with a certain essence elucidates this being in the same manner. Either something is a human being or not, and correspondingly its expressions human or not. Nonetheless there are varying degrees in the arrangement in the development of an essence's powers. On the basis of the greatest amount of influence we measure the meaning that applies to manifestations of capacities that are less fully developed although still present. In order to grasp the real human import of a skeleton from the lower Pleistocene, we inevitably draw parallels to later products of technology and return from there to the previous forms. (Of course, there is also the converse procedure in which we attempt to illuminate the present forms of modern culture through the life-

style of prehistoric human beings, as A. Gehlen does. This procedure builds on the former one and confirms in this manner its basic function.) In the case of technological production we may naturally assume that the same goals are present (e.g., cutting something) and are merely achieved through different and variously proficient means (bone splinters or laser beams). One can tell from a *good* cutting tool what a cutting tool is *in general.*

Can this model be transposed to human beings? Yes, if human beings can be defined in terms of specific achievements (products). The better the achievements are, the more one can distinguish in what humanity consists from the human being who is capable of executing and does execute such actions. This conception (developed by Aristotle) must be supplemented by the consideration that with the emergence of extremely great possibilities the darker counterpossibilities also come into existence or become more clear. It appears — aside from the technological area — problematic to rate achievements according to their degree of excellence. Is the family of the Stone Age lower in every respect to that of the late Middle Ages in Europe, and according to which standard should "lower" and "higher" be measured here? Can it be decided somehow whether the Greek language at the time of Homer better expressed the essence of language than modern Greek? That hardly appears possible. For our purposes, however, it is not important to claim a gradation of realizations of essences but rather to prepare the conceptual means for managing extreme differences in the development of human beings *in case* such differences occur. At any rate, there is something to be said for making this assumption if one considers the testimony left behind by the myriad epochs of the history of human beings, back to the dark beginnings. As soon as we move back beyond the fringe of the Neolithic revolution (approximately 10,000 B.C.) in which the basic features of our present culture were laid, it becomes more difficult for us not only to gather an idea of human life at this time but also to determine the basic features of humanity that remain throughout the changes of time.

2. UNIVERSALITY OF COMPREHENSION?

40. At this point a new difficulty arises. We are aiming for a definition of the essence of human beings that gathers central features of humanity together such that we can locate these features in a relatively identical sense in all human beings that we know. However, we construct this concept mainly from our own realm of experiences, that of a Western academic milieu in the second half of the twentieth century. Even if we attempt to recur to general human experience, we shall not succeed completely—as will be evident to others and our successors—in capturing the general aspects from the peculiarities of our experiences. The concept we have formed, albeit with the best intentions for objectivity, cannot simply be taken over by those living in different situations as a finished product—not even if one cannot accuse our work of bias, mistakes, or incoherence. Because every philosopher and every circle of philosophers is grasping for the truth from a particular place in the roots of one's thought, it is possible for them to stand behind whatever they believe to have found out while still not identifying this knowledge with the truth to such an extent that they would only have to hand it down without any changes so that the next generation would possess the truth. Rather, philosophical knowledge can only be handed down productively, and the instigator must also want this change.

41. Negative forms of this attitude would be, on the one hand, egocentrism (or ethnocentrism) and, on the other hand, relativism. Ethnocentrism, which seems to correspond to a natural tendency in human groups—many primitive tribes call themselves "the human beings," views its own contingent social, technological, and other institutions (habits,

views, forms of organization) as being properly human. Measured against this norm, the institutions of other groups, seen
as a whole, are inferior ("wild," "childish," "animalistic"),
although one may recognize specific points of equality or
even superiority. From this the belief can result that it is necessary or at least legitimate to bring the proper culture to
these peoples, which most often implies that they must be
oppressed militarily and politically. Egocentrism holds the
same principle, only on a smaller scale. Relativism is a way
out of the naive arrogance which leads to egoism. Relativism is the idea that all attitudes and opinions of different
cultures and individuals have equal validity. In fact, the relativist can accept anything because the questions to which
various answers are available have become uninteresting. He
can be tolerant because he does not take seriously the claim
of truth for life. In this manner, however, he will do justice
to neither those who think differently nor himself because
he judges himself and others as too insignificant. Additionally, one can only be a relativist in those areas that are (really or putatively) irrelevant to life. The generosity of the
relativist ends where considerations are at hand that are in-
separably tied with the skeptic's vital interests or basic attitude toward humanity.

42. Neither the ideological elevation of one's own perspective toward the truth nor the attempt of jumping from
one's own perspective into a reciprocal modification of all
possible perspectives solves our problem. Both falsely assume
that it must be possible to have and formulate an absolute
truth in objective knowledge such that the differences between the knowledge-seeking subjects yield to the unity of
a single subject. Thus, even if there are several numerically
different subjects, in reference to whatever, and how, they
claim to be true, they are one, a single ("transcendental")
subject. This demand is reasonable if—as is the case in
mathematics—the norms for the acceptance of knowledge
as such have been and could be laid down in a binding manner because the object of knowledge does not belong to the

practical self-understanding of the knowing human being in the same way as it does in the case of our anthropological question. In reference to the knowledge of truth in its complete and unreduced depth and meaningfulness for life, the different concreteness of truth-seeking subjects is constitutive; it is neither possible nor meaningful to eliminate them.

43. From these considerations proceeds the illumination of the necessity and difficulty of conversation in which real progress toward self-knowledge of the center of humanity can occur. Such a discussion in which the supraindividuality of the eternal concrete truth is to be evident is something different than a discussion of theses and, of course, something different than an exchange of experiences, although it must contain such elements as well. This is especially true for discussions between our scientific rational culture and those cultures structured around "myths." It is clear that this discussion, just as difficult as it is necessary for the future of humanity, cannot take place—as it almost always has in the past—on the basis and with the norms of the one, rationally thinking partner if it is to be fertile. This discussion is increasingly becoming one of the most important "places" in anthropological knowledge in reference to a comprehensive humanistic world culture in which the "rational" and "mythical" elements of our in principle Western culture can perhaps achieve greater synthesis.

B. Basic Dimensions of Human Existence

44. In order to describe the peculiarity of human being-in-the-world, human subjectivity, it is reasonable to determine the essential features of this existence. Similarly to how a body extends essentially over the three dimensions of geometrical space, human existence—the encountering, the world, and the individual act of being—lives in certain dimensions through which the kind and degree of its existence are given. The following basic dimensions are to be considered: language proficiency, sociality, historicity, and bodiliness. Because these dimensions are only conceptually—as aspects—and not really distinct and because their distinction cannot be derived from some higher principle from which they could be shown to be an exhaustive list, we are talking, not about "the" basic dimensions, but rather only—indeterminately intended—about some basic dimensions.

45. However, it is not merely intuitive that these dimensions, present in every human existence, are basic and constitutive for the peculiarity of humans. A further reason for this claim is that these features do not only determine the existence of humans but are also noticeable—more often than

not destructive—basic features of anthropological reflection itself when such reflection is within the horizon of the ideal of objective knowledge: as the fact that every human search for one's essence is invariably determined in part by one's concrete historical place, social problems, linguistic culture, and so on. Finally, we can extract a hint as to the basic character of the mentioned dimensions from the fact that each of the sciences that correspond to each dimension has claimed for itself the status of being *the* basic human science. Thus, one developed—in so-called "structuralism"—the idea that the humanities were to be reformed according to the model of structural linguistics; one called and calls what raises human beings above mere "naturalness," in the one case, "society," and in another case, "history"; and one expects from the social or historical science the decisive illumination of humanity in general. Of course, these claims that occasionally even occur as sole representative claims are a matter of changing fashion. Nevertheless, one cannot deny these sciences the right of thematizing essential dimensions of human existence that permeate each other in subject matter, although they can be separate in analysis. For us these claims only represent hints anyway. Thus, we need not be concerned that the particular dimensions are not claimed with equal emphasis to be the basic structures of human existence and that bodiliness which certainly does constitute one basic dimension of human existence does not really fit that well into our schema: To what extent is bodiliness a basic feature of the anthropological search for knowledge itself? Can one understand the different sciences of human beings as perhaps a part of medicine without invoking an act of violence?

46. Our basic dimensions define the "subject matter" of different human sciences. Therefore, the thematization of these basic dimensions must take place in conjunction with the human sciences—naturally not with each on their own terrain on which special problems can be dealt with along with the assumption of certain methods and "paradigmata"

(Th. S. Kuhn) but rather in the intermediary places in which the sciences repeatedly come when there is a controversy about leading models, approaches, and so on. In such cases the distinctions and relations between theory and praxis, subject matter and theory, that appear to have been cleared up in favor of certain determinations for concrete research programs become problematic again. Philosophers, especially anthropological philosophers, enter into this area in their own way: by learning how to notice in what medium they, living and thinking, are already moving: in indeterminate, inevitable, but still contingent conditions that internally determine one's life and thought. The structure of these conditions are objectively researched (e.g., from linguistics, sociology, etc.); the conditioned existence of our subjective life reveals itself in a kind of reflection in which we have inner access to it. From this reflection it can be established that the methodologically basic feature of the human sciences is hermeneutics, the interpretation of the dimensions of lived life in light of its natural structures, whereby the living person brings his own assumptions clearly to his awareness. Correspondingly, our philosophical conversation with the human sciences has a different character than that with the natural sciences. Whereas with the latter the humane appeared as a kind of living organism in addition to others or as something different than ourselves, whereas in the former we meet it as the structuring complex that is each and every one of us. Still, this complex can be characterized to a larger extent as something different (relative to us) than it can for the case of the inner dynamics which we will thematize in the transcendental considerations in Part C.

I. Language

47. "The human being is the only animal that has the gift of speech (logos)" and, thus, reason. This statement of Aristotle (*Politics* 1,2 1253a 10) that found its classical expression in the Latin form "homo est animal rationale" is still true today. Still, what do linguistic capacities mean for human beings? General linguistics and linguistic philosophy that, by the way, have an unusual and wide horizon can contribute to an answer to this question.

1. SPEECH ACTS AND LANGUAGE SYSTEMS

48. In the most varying conversations, discussions, and such, certain elements arise again and again: whole sentences, expressions, words, word stems, and sounds. The occurrence of these elements allows for many combinations, albeit determined by certain rules. By means of observation it is possible to study the collection of elements and rules that belong to our language by forming lists of these forms and rules and looking to see whether any kind of system underlies these lists. From this collection, called language, one can interpret conversations, discussions, and so on as certain acts that come into existence via the use of the possibilities in this collection. With this the distinction, basic for linguistics, is drawn between language (language system) and speech acts (de Saussure: *langue/parole*).

49. The elements of language—that one can denote with "symbol" with regards to the meaning function of speech —stand in a more or less systematic connection with one another whose structure can be studied. Since a language system can change historically, one must distinguish the synchronic mode of observation (that refers to the state of a language at a certain point in time) from the diachronic mode (that represents the change in a language over time). Because this change does not depend completely on external factors, one must distinguish between the basic structure of a language and the factual structure of a language at a certain point in time (Chomsky: surface and deep structure).

Because there is not just one language but rather very many and basically different languages in which (essentially) the same content is expressed with completely different signs, one will try to find the structure that underlies the inner structure of all languages—partially in order to have a neutral basis for comparison and partially in order to come closer to the essence of language.

50. One of the most important results of this approach is the insight that every language is a hierarchically ordered system of differences. Thus, it is possible to formulate different messages and even an infinite number of different messages with very few signs of the first order and relatively few signs of the second order, and so on. The principle of difference states that the meaning of a certain sign lies in the fact that it distinguishes itself from other signs of the same system which could stand in a certain place in a complex just as easily by conveying differing messages.

Every language system is a hierarchical layering of systems. When we refer to the basic form of linguistic use, spoken discourse, we see that because "m" and "h" are two different *phonemes* in English, we can attribute different meanings to the expressions "hat" and "mat." Phonemes are different and more than merely voiced noises. They are the acoustic elements of a *language.* Thus the difference in the phonemes does not lie solely on the acoustic level but rather is determined by a phonological system that is peculiar to each language. s/ß is, despite the acoustic difference, only one phoneme in German (*sonne* = *ßonne*), whereas in English they are two (sue ≠ zoo). The difference in phonemes whose number ranges, depending on the language, between 22 and 36 becomes relevant for meanings on the level of *monemes* (which is approximately equivalent to a word along with all of its grammatical family members). Still, an isolated word, much less an isolated inflection ending, has no meaning alone; it has to be, implicitly or explicitly, part of a *sentence*. The meaning that it retains independently of the sentence can be a possible element of other possible sentences in addition to this one. However, a sentence has no clear meaning if it is not related to a *context* with other sentences of speech situations (as an example compare the same sentence in a grammar book and in a real life context, and the latter in different situations or with a different emphasis, and so on).

51. Meanings do not have any particular, intrinsic linguistic sign. Nothing has a name in itself that is like the name we have given it, and no sign (in its material constitution) has any natural relation to its object (with the exception of the relatively few cases of onomatopoeia). The principle of difference still only explains how a sign has a *different* meaning than another one, but not how it can have a meaning at all, that is, how a linguistic sign can ever come into existence as such. Yet we have determined that linguistic signs only have their meaning in real, life-contextual positing, that is, the living speech act. Language (as a collection, *langue*) and speech acts (*parole*) are prior to one another in different respects. Without a real language no differentiated speech acts could develop; there would be only a very few signs (sounds, gestures, etc.), not hierarchically ordered or only so to a small extent, that would be naturally formed and understood, that is, the small circle of communication systems of other primates. On the other hand, a language system — if we disregard the point that it is only formed

through speech — is nothing but a capacity of bringing forth certain sound configurations or marks on paper unless there is reference to effective understanding. Thus, it would seem that speech acts receive a certain priority *within* the dialectic relationship of both moments.

2. ACHIEVEMENTS OF LANGUAGE

52. We can see what language achieves in speech acts. What really happens in speech acts? This question is generally dealt with under the title of the "functions" of language. Different lists of these functions are given (see Keller 1979, 43–45). Since we are not concerned with an exhaustive or acceptable classification of these functions but rather only with the principle aspect of the linguistic (co)constitution of the human world, we can limit ourselves to relying on the classical division. The psychologist Karl Bühler (1934, 28) distinguished three functions of language: symbol (representation of states of affairs), symptom (proclamation of inner states of the speaker), and signal (appeal to the hearer from whom a certain reaction is expected). These functions can also be formulated as such: presentation of the discussed topic, self-realization of the speaking subject, communication between subjects. With these formulations we are picking up on our "definition" of subjectivity: a relation to oneself in our behavior toward others. What should be apparent is that language determines the act of subjectivity according to its three functions. We proceed such that we confront successful cases of communication with faulty modes of communication that are due to a lack of linguistic ability or a hindrance of its execution. When the effective power of something is the issue, we must take the highest achievements into account and, at the same time, those achievements that occur when the capacity in question is deficient.

a) Presentation

53. The presence of something does not first come into existence through language but rather is taken over and ordered by it. This "something" or "state of affairs" can have differing basic modes and correspondingly different modes of presence. Accordingly, very different modes of linguistic presentation are to be distinguished. In the following only *one* such line is to be drawn out, starting from a simple case of sense perception that is articulated in sentence form.

54. The basic level of sense perception is already linguistic. The simple perceptive act that the table is brown already has a propositional structure. In this structure something is already determined first as a table and then as brown. The determination itself is executed with the help of the meanings "table" and "brown" that are taken with specific meanings from the English language. If our attention is fixed on a certain perceptual field that is outlined roughly linguistically, then it can be further ordered, which will, once again, be a linguistic function: via correct interpretation and talk the perceptual act comes to completion; one sees, smells, and hears correctly only when this has happened. Of course, one can talk something to death or mask it verbosely. Still, a musically educated person can hear one of Beethoven's quartets better than someone who does not know what a fugue or an inversion is. Musical education is not mediated solely through language, but the teaching and learning in the medium of language plays a central role.

55. Language allows us to go beyond the essential function of presenting things present to presenting things not present or not anymore. In other words, the capacity to remember what one has experienced and the capacity to anticipate what one might yet experience, and, thus, all planning and practical considerations, do not exactly become possible linguistically, but they are at least coconstituted through language in their breadth, sharpness, and objectivity. Without narra-

tive—a linguistic form—what one could remember would decay into chance and associative threads of memory, and there would be no stories or even continuous connection of stories which could constitute history—either my past or the past of a people. The same is true for fantastic anticipated experiences or for possible experiences that take place in novels, and so on. The interlacing of several means-ends relationships is characteristic for planning; to be aware of such a complex is hardly possible without linguistic means. The basic fact that the space for memories and remembering is extended through linguistic information beyond the borders of my personal experiences and memories to "the" past and to "what happens" everywhere is contained in all of the preceding.

56. Even if everything which is absent lay in the realm of what is, in principle, sensually present or capable of being experienced, theories would contribute to our awareness things which cannot be present for us other than in a linguistic way: the curvature of space in the universe, the emergence of a neurosis, the coherence of an explanation, the truth of a statement, and so on. All of those things which theories illuminate would never have been in view without language. We are not talking about what is already apparent, but rather, speaking in a certain way, we make reality familiar to ourselves. Of course, one can—in a different way—cover up reality. However, this is only possible because the apparent reality is linguistically mediated in states of affairs.

57. Finally, language, in the sense of lying beyond what is directly spoken and in contrast to this too immediate understanding, can allow for the presence of something that is never objectively real. Speaking normally has a certain ambiguity that has a positive function. In literature, and especially in poetry, one moves in a kind of ambiguity that—as long as the essential function is to remain intact—cannot be reduced to a determinate piece of information (what would happen if one were to read the letters literally or simply tran-

scribe what the metaphorical description stood for?). In a poem the ambiguity of the appearing reality becomes apparent, in a deceiving or abysmal sense. The essence is *between* the lines, metaphorically speaking—but also between *lines* that are ordered in a certain way. If one does not succeed in finding the correct poetic language, an important mode of presence of ineffability, perhaps presence in general, is eliminated. (Naturally the reverse is also true—which is not our subject matter—that true poetic language cannot emerge in a mental desert that is experienced and taken as such.) It is possible that the poetically ambiguous form of spoken language with its magical power is not only an artistic blooming but also the beginning form of speaking at all from which the normal, daily, and scientific use of language arose through banalization and narrowing without being able to lose its origin completely.

b) Communication

58. The increased attention given to nonverbal communication in recent years (see, e.g., Fast 1970) should not hide the fact that human communication is most often identical with the fact that one speaks with one another. What one could say if one were limited to the "vocabulary" of prelinguistic modes of communication would be quite minimal— about as much as the "language" of highly developed animals allows for. The case is quite different when human beings capable of language consciously limit themselves to nonverbal communication or when deaf people communicate with one another. In the latter cases one still speaks from a linguistically interpreted world: on the one hand, consciously renouncing speech (which is only possible when one is talking with oneself) and, on the other hand, in deaf sign language developed and taught by normal-speaking people. What would we know about the world of another if she did not talk? Even a strong capacity of placing oneself in another's perspective or a sharp talent for observation (from

whose linguistic mediation one is to abstract) quickly reach limits that can only be transgressed through linguistic revelation by the other. Human beings that talk to one another share a part of life with one another, be it banally or in conflict.

59. This is not only true for the interim. The world in which various individual worlds cross over is only constituted through the exchange of opinions and knowledge. Contracts of all kinds (marriage, work, national contracts, etc.) have the form of certain linguistic events. The same is true for legal and other judgments. The organization of social life occurs so that one talks about others, over another's head, for a position, around an issue, and so on. New functions require new names for their establishment. One constitutes —linguistically—new uses of language (expressly or nonexpressly, an insider jargon or a technical terminology) and, thus, creates new forms of community and communication (to which the exclusion of others belongs: even in the oppression-free talk of philosophers only those who keep to the rules of discourse are admitted). More comprehensive and longer-lasting forms of cooperation are inconceivable without language; after a certain point of differentiation (since the beginning of city cultures and everything that belongs to them) it is not possible without the development of language in a written form.

60. Language is one of the most basic social institutions. It is, as the product and expression of a common existence, the primary means of maintaining and creating new relations. As a social institution it is largely removed from the volition of individuals. Not until a human child grows into a linguistic society does it become aware of itself to an extent where it is capable of volition: personal thought and decision that can then even decide against its own foundation: against the common language and the linguistically mediated society. Before a human being belongs to himself, he is "expropriated," for he only receives his possessions from a language and a linguistic community. This is true not only

for one's native language in general but also for one's dialect and for certain coined phrases (proverbs, legal maxims, articles of faith, etc.) that retain a fixed form in varying contexts similar to words in sentences and constitute a higher system of signs in which the difference between the form (sign collection) and the content (the message) can only be drawn to a limited extent. This shows clearly that a language is closely connected with the particular life-world in which it is spoken. This is true for the language of a fisher in a coastal Indian village as it is for English in an international airport.

61. Because language is essentially a social phenomenon, institutional differences in caste within a society must be made linguistically. An apprentice speaks differently to her equals than to her boss; the hunter who accompanies the king on a hunt cannot speak of "we"; in many languages (such as German and French) where there is a difference between the formal and informal second personal pronoun (you), there are often embarrassing situations; in some linguistic families (e.g., the Javanian) one must use almost completely different vocabularies according to the degree of difference to the addressee. Despite these linguistically fixed caste and class differences there remains a large degree of linguistic elements in common, so that one is somehow impressed when an outsider sees that the upper and lower classes can understand each other in the same language and, thus, have something in common prior to any demarcation or any express search for similarities.

c) Self-realization in Expression

62. How important it is for a child to be addressed regarding its personal and other possibilities and to continue to be addressed in these respects — encouragement, feedback, teaching, and so on — is clear to anyone who considers what happens if this does not occur, occurs in a reversed order, or is experienced successfully. It is just as important, however, that the addressee find an appropriate answer or, to be

more general, can express what moves her internally. We have a large variety of means of expressions; language is one of them that stands in the limelight so much that the others enjoy being called "language" metaphorically. Thus, one can speak of the language of music, dance, pantomime, and even psychosomatic symptoms. It seems as if one uses the expression "language" foremost for those means of expression whose use (as a language) must be learned, and only derivatively for those modes of expression that are innately natural and spontaneous.

63. I can express a pain with a grimace, an inarticulate groan and cry; then I am expressing myself in an innate, universal language, albeit subject to my free will. As soon as I—as an American or Englishman—cry "Ouch!" scream and language are connected, since in other languages it is "Au!" or "Ai!" or whatever. The expression "It hurts!" is more accentuated, and "I have a stomachache!" is even more accentuated. The medium of expression shows a greater resistance to the meaning to be expressed because of its own uninhibited individuality. "Ouch!" can hardly be true or false; it is a way of speaking in which no grammatical or stylistic mistakes can be made, but also no special effects can be achieved either as is the case for linguistic forms of expression: as in the sentences just mentioned and to a greater extent by dirges such as that of King Hezekiah (Isaiah book 38, 10–16) or of Gretchen in *Faust* ("My peace is gone" verses 3374–3413).

64. The point of the great dirges is, most often, not only physical pain. If this can be expressed with an "Ouch!"-cry, then the pain (as well as joy) of love of another human being, of her people and home, and of her God requires expression through words. Of course, dance, choir, and sculptural creation can play a large role—but never without reference to linguistic conception, interpretation, and supplementation. These means of expression are neglected too much in our "head"-oriented culture—as it appears in favor of linguistic expression. If we take a closer look, however, it is

not that language *per se* dominates other forms of expression, but the objectifying observation language of the type "I have problems with my stomach, relationship, or life!" This narrowed language can gain depth, density, and fullness through reference to the other means of expression. Thus, one can see that nonlinguistic means of expression form an indivisible unity with language. This unity stands the test in the highest intellectual heights. Many, like Kleist, can only come to progressive thought while walking; others must have a pencil to think on paper; yet others can only think creatively if they have to explain something to others and, thus, give the ideas the possibility of mingling in the flow of speech. Is it not also the case that during a lecture the tone, the accompanying gestures, and imponderable resonance mediates as much as the text one can have printed out in front of oneself, robbed of its liveliness? Especially the converse is true: no gesture, sublime as it may be, can express what Hölderlin expressed in his later hymns or Hegel in his *Phenomenology of Spirit*.

65. Namely what? What did Hölderlin and Hegel express? What we can read. Whatever is to be expressed receives its ordered existence only through expressions—not only for others but also for the poet and philosopher. Of course, they carried something in themselves previously which they then proceeded to express according to the rules of a certain poetic type or a certain philosophical argumentative structure. However, this form ordered not only the expression but also the inner content: the thoughts and, to a certain extent, the feelings. What we see in these particular cases is important for stating the principle. Linguistic expression is something very differentiated, even in relatively primitive modes of communication and without taking stylistic elements into consideration. By expressing ourselves through these modes we differentiate our inner states retroactively. This is true for humanity as such as contrasted with prehuman beings. It is also true for imprecisely speaking and, thus, imprecisely thinking human beings as contrasted with original formu-

lating and subtly perceiving human beings. That differentiations are not constructed in a decaying linguistic culture, but rather are confused or hindered from emerging, is not an argument to the contrary, but rather the negative case of the principle at hand.

66. By familiarizing ourselves with forms of expression, and that centrally in language, we develop our possibilities; we become ourselves. Whatever is not expressed either lies fallow or searches for an outlet. It is often the case that human beings become ill if, for whatever reason, they do not adequately express themselves or do not have the courage to do so. Therefore, it is a basic need of almost all human beings to talk about themselves. Thus, conversation is one of the central elements of therapy, especially psychotherapy. The French psychoanalyst Jacques Lacan (d. 1981) even went so far as to define recovery from a psychological illness as the liberation of the word (*libération de la parole*).

3. LANGUAGE AS MEANS AND AS MEDIATION

67. When speaking (and hearing) adequately fulfills its function of mediating the presence of things, persons, and oneself normally, it does not reach awareness itself. One becomes aware of the reality of language mostly when the function of mediation is hindered or when it succeeds in an excellent and surprising way. The loss of achievement—in what the concrete way of speaking withholds—makes manifest what language achieves on its most basic level and in its best exemplification. However, this also makes manifest that this mediation achievement occurs through something which has its own reality apart from the message to be mediated.

In the following we shall sketch four situations in which language appears to be an endangered means of mediation. We shall orient our examples foremost on the function of presentation.

68. (1) In *lying* the trust that we normally have toward

what is spoken—that it tells us the truth—is misused. As soon as we are aware of this, the dependability of the spoken is, in principle, shaken: there can also be "false" sentences. Thus, the converse problem arises as to how a linguistic complex can be true at all. If a sentence is only viewed as a grammatical unit and not as a claim about a state of affairs, the problem becomes insoluble. One must, conversely, assume the relationship of language to truth—which is really quite mysterious!—and then interpret falsity as an unequal, deprived mode of truth-reference whose falsity is hardly possible without the linguistic sentential form of our knowledge reference.

69. (2) Encasement of language use: because words we use are worn out, wander too far away from their intention, or are plagued with banal supplementary meanings because one uses too many "sophisticated" words of whose meaning one is not really clear, because metaphors are driven out of use: because of these and similar reasons reality appears only approximate, without pregnant contours, without colors, and as if it were made out of paper. The words do not have any "grip" anymore; our reference to reality becomes uncertain and thin, just as it is in the converse case. In a sense *au contraire* the linguistic coconstitution of the reference to reality becomes clear—along with the implications that result for an ethics of speaking.

70. (3) The experience with speech that is directed toward me in a *foreign language* can stem from two different situations: according to whether I understand this language well or poorly.

If I master the language of another only poorly, my relation to the world that is mediated through it does not always function properly. Time and time again I must stop and think or ask what this or that expression means. That is, the mediation is interrupted; what mediates can become the thematically discussed means. As long as the expressions are the objects of attention they do not mediate. If, however, I understand the foreign language very well, it will become thematic for me for quite a different reason: I become aware that what is spoken in one language can only be inadequately translated into what is spoken in another. Every language turns out to be special; each has its own interpretation pattern that stands in an indivisible connection with the life-world of the community in which it is spoken and understood. (Comparative linguistic research deals with these facts: see v. Humboldt 1830/35, Whorf 1956, Gipper 1987.) Nothing has a name in and of itself as it has in our language.

71. (4) Spoken language can become *foreign until it is only a group of sounds.* This can occur in very different situations and correspondingly different ways: sounds carry over from a neighboring room to me; is someone speaking? I hear people speaking a foreign language and am awed at its rich melody. A child pronounces a word very articulately (i.e., "h-o-u-s-e") and cannot find anything similar to a house in the sequence of the sounds. One experiences in these cases that the spoken linguistic signs—with the limited exceptions of onomatopoeia—are conventional and have no intrinsic relationship to the meanings that they in fact have. No configuration of sounds (or black marks on paper) means anything in and of itself, and nothing has a name written on its forehead.

72. What is spoken and what reveals itself are thus—in any particular case and in principle—only factually, and not essentially, identical, only through contingent mediation and not immediately. They are still one in successful and in "unhappy" cases. The above sentences, that nothing has a name as it does in our language or means anything in and of itself, are to be set in dialectic opposition to Stefan George's sentence "Where word breaks off no thing may be" (Heidegger 1971, 57–108).

Thus, the naive experience of an identity of language and the world—the world as a magical linguistic paradise—is not only to be disrupted by the discovery of a plurality of languages and the nonnaturalness of the function of signs, but one must also banish the danger of an extrinsic technomor-

phic understanding of language that quickly follows the former discovery.

73. All originality can only be interpreted with the means
of what has been previously created; in this manner it is successful and misses the point at the same time. As regards
original language this role is played by written, second (foreign), artificial, and logically normative scientific languages.
We have before us a development of language that itself functions as language. Here we have before us the elements and
rules of combination for a language, objectively present and
— as far as it is an artificial language or notational system —
constructively transparent. The concepts "linguistic sign,"
"sign system," "code," and so on stem from this context. The
interpretation of language according to the model of elec-
tronic news technology and the transformation of language
for the purpose of increasingly comprehensive "communication" (along with the corresponding Romanticist reactions
that call for originality) describe in their connections the way
in which language is increasingly available to us today. There
is also no way of changing that. One should remain aware,
however, that the theory of language that grows out of an
analysis of written words with the help of terminology stemming from the realm of artificial languages can only provide
a model that arises through the projection of the former's
concepts and functions onto the vaguely accessible, actually spoken language of the first order. Nothing is actually
"coded" in language of the first order, because it belongs to
the nature of coding that the message to be translated is already present (in a linguistic form) and that the code is not
available in a clear arrangement. Both assumptions are not
true in this case: a code becomes something secondary, a
translation process into another language, through the primary formulation; and that our native language is present
as an objectified code (in the grammar and dictionary, etc.)
is a very late fact in the history of culture that is to a large
extent irrelevant for actual speaking. In this manner we are
always confronted with language secondarily. Basically, it

is more and different than a tool that we use to attain certain goals (the transmission of certain messages). It has "essentially grown up with human beings," a "secret never to be found out completely" (W. v. Humboldt). Language has a constitutive function for the constitution of the world of human beings.

II. Sociality

74. If language is one of the most basic social institutions and if its manifestation is normally an exchange between two people, then there is a natural transition from considerations concerning language to a thematization of the sociality of human existence. Belonging to ordered groups of people and communicating to others are essential features of each particular human being. To have and develop this insight, and from the place from which we stand, thinking philosophically, is the task of the following. Because thinking is a personal, individuating act, we are not thematizing the structure of societies, but rather the significance of existence in society and of encounters for each individual. Because the mode of socialization of human beings displays great differences in the myriad cultures and epochs of humanity, an abstract, general proposition about sociality, not only in particular cases but also in broad strokes, could only be achieved at the price of extreme generality. It would be gained, however, at the cost of losing the character of the reflection intended to be characteristic of our considerations. For this reason we refer to the forms of sociality in our present culture that are to be elucidated for their essential features. We have chosen the expression "sociality" or "social relation" because the expressions "life in a community, society, group, common essence, relationship, and so on" already denote special modes of "socialness," whereas in our line of questioning we are concerned with a word that is neutral toward all of these special modes.

1. THE PHENOMENON OF THE SOCIAL

75. That every human being lives in some—even very manifold—mode of sociality with other human beings is a universal fact. Before we ask why that is the case—that is, what meaning it has—we must secure an overview of the variety of social relations. The fact that the numerous and colorful social relations do not have to be brought into order retrospectively by an observer, but rather that almost all of them grow out of a certain order (from a relatively stable structure of relational tracks, from a network of standardized interactions and interaction possibilities) is fortunate for us. These structures stand in a similar relation to the particular social relations as language does to the particular speech acts. In this manner they can be studied or reconstructed just as the various language systems can be studied.

76. Social systems that overlap in manifold ways can be listed: family, relatives, friends, town, professional group, work associates, neighbors, church community, class, state, and so on. One sees immediately that one belongs to a family differently than to a state, to a small town at the turn of the century differently than to a small neighborhood of a contemporary urban community, to a group of steelworkers or librarians, to an American parish or a Brazilian base group—irrespective of the particular way in which each person lives his relationship in these communities. In order to grasp these different senses of community, one often refers to certain contrasts like those between naturally developed and arbitrarily founded communities, between stable and labile, between self-oriented and goal-oriented, between partnership and hierarchically constructed communities. These differences are fruitful for the characterization and classification of social relations as long as one remains aware that they are artificial constructs. In reality, one will often find that a social system, for example, is *more likely* to be described as self-oriented and goal-oriented, without definitively being able to assign it to one type while excluding the

others; the same is true for the other differences mentioned.
77. Relations between human beings take place, not in vacuums of indeterminate possibilities, but rather in the space of expectations, roles, and so on that is previously determined to a certain extent by the position of the related partners in a community, whether it be in a relatively lasting way (husband, father, teacher, taxpayer, neighbor) or in a temporary manner (current president, neighbor on the bench, referee). Even the relationship of "one on one" is not formless— especially when they are introduced with these words but also in any other case. With whom, when, in which way, and to what extent this aspect can and should influence the relationship lies structurally prior to our capabilities and volition according to the nature of the matter as it is interpreted in our culture. If there were not such immanent structures of relations, we could not be able to study them abstractly or claim them to be true and original reality. The relations would be nothing more than the changing copresence at certain space-time places, and its network would have the significance and consistency of Brownian molecular movement, that is, either zero or very limited.

These structures do not merely support the particular relations objectively as a pattern, but the human beings that relate to each other through them relate to these structures as well (and in a sense prior thereto). The mode, the positive or negative tone, the degree of *identification* with the patterns that are given by membership to a social group influence the relations deeply. The social, human being is related to herself by being related to others. More precisely, she is related to her own existential possibilities that are encouraged by the expectations of others who are, once again, socially influenced—and this is how she is related to the expectant person and, at the same time, to the social arena in which the encounter occurs.

78. The relations can be of differing quality: relations of cooperation or conflict; the relation can be characterized by indifference or interest (love, hate, etc.); there are assignments

of equality, dominance, and inferiority of all kinds: one-sided, two-sided, and many-sided relations—in order to name only several viewpoints for noting the rich palette of phenomena. It is not our task to give a comprehensive classification of social phenomena. For our purposes it suffices to waken an awareness of the manifold of the inner structure of social reality before its human significance is philosophically explained.

2. SOCIOBIOLOGY, SOCIOLOGY, SOCIAL PHILOSOPHY

The possibility and significance of such a philosophical explanation is attacked by some. What task remains for the philosophy of the social if there is already sociology? Further, what significance can social philosophy and sociology, taken together, have in light of the claims of sociobiology? Let's begin with the latter difficulty since it is more comprehensive.

79. Sociobiology is a theory of social phenomena on the basis of biology, or more precisely: the population genetic interpretation of animal behavior. Population is defined as "the community of potentially endogenous individuals in a certain geographical space" (Vogel-Angermann 1980, 457). Every animal that can sexually reproduce has, on the average, half of its genes in common with its siblings, one-fourth with its "nieces" and "nephews," an eighth with its "cousins," and so on. If one assumes (see Wickler-Seibt 1977, 296f.) that the objective goal toward which all animal behavior strives in the end is survival, reproduction, and propagation of its genes, then "egoistic" and "altruistic behavior" of the animal becomes understandable, namely, as a variation (determined by the situation) of the strategy through which the genes follow their invariable egoistic goals. In this manner one cannot only explain why a lion who "marries" a lioness widow with cubs often will bite to death the offspring of

his predecessor in order to secure better survival chances for his own cubs, but one can also explain why a rabbit does not immediately run away from an approaching dog, but rather stomps on the ground to warn his fellow rabbits despite running a larger risk itself. This genetically programmed behavior only represents a danger for the rabbit's genes insofar as the genes are in this rabbit; it is advantageous insofar as they are found in related rabbits in the group, which is, on the average, greater than in the individual; three siblings of one individual represent one and one-half times the gene pool of the individual. In a similar way one can understand why "nature" forces most of the female bees to forgo reproduction and use their care and nourishment for the queen sisters and their offspring (Wilson 1980, 19; see Lévi-Strauss 1981, 368). In this manner one approximates more closely the constitutive laws of the social formation of bees, wasps, and ants that are equipped with chromosome pools of haplodiploids. Seen in principle, a path is cleared to the causes of social institutions in general.

80. One can attempt to partially explain human social behavior in this manner as well. The touching smile of a three-month-old infant, the unjust harshness of stepfathers and stepmothers, the sacrificial death of the fireman: all of that has its objective utility for the future of certain gene pools that determine behavior in accord with their "interests." Of course, sociobiologists see that not all behavior can be explained immediately through heredity and in the light of genetic propagation; the present modes of cultural behavior taken over through imitation are too various and removed from nature, at least since the quicker rhythm of cultural differentiation overtook the slow rhythm of biological evolution and very clearly since the neolithic revolution. Nonetheless, ethnological and sociological understanding must—according to many sociobiologists—let biological understanding have its place in the end, because "no species, ours included, has a meaning or goal that extends beyond the commands created in its genetic history" (Wilson 1980,

10). Thus, for example, the brain exists "because it promotes the survival and reproduction that controls its constitution. The human mind is a means of survival and reproduction, and reason is only one of its various techniques" (ibid.). It is clear that the construction of the biological is enriched (in this case) through materialistic premises that force him to reject all philosophy as unscientific because his science has secretly become a philosophy. For the thesis that there can be no real qualitative evolution—an emergence of truly novel and higher forms—because on the level of biochemistry and genetics one abstracts from these dimensions, is, of course, a thesis that is to be discussed philosophically. It is, however, also clear that the sociobiologist must claim that sociologists can only provide "limited descriptions of superficial phenomena" (Wilson 1980, 9) whose deep structure only the sociobiologist can know.

81. That some modes of social behavior for human beings are genetically programmed has been shown to be quite probable by research in ethology (see, e.g., Eibl-Eibesfeldt 1972). To what extent behavior is really innate and to what extent it is attained or modified culturally is a question plagued by many uncertainties for which progressive research will find a discriminating answer. Whether the factor of heredity or the factor of learning will prove to be more powerful, seen for the totality of human behavior, cannot be decided at this point. At any rate, it appears to be the case that genetic explanation needs the theoretical explanation provided by learning as a supplement. A theory that does not receive its contours from other alternatives, that is, that sees confirmation of itself in certain phenomena as well as their opposites, explains anything and, therefore, nothing. For it has foregone the possibility of falsification which is essential for scientific theories and becomes—in the bad sense of the word—metaphysical. As a statement about the ultimate structure of living organisms that slips into favoring the term nature within the phenomenal difference between nature and culture, necessity and freedom, and so on, it be-

comes entangled in the dilemma that will be discussed in the chapters on "body" and "freedom": if everything, including our mental actions, is genetically programmed in the sense of an irrevocable positing of purpose, then there is no significance in holding sociobiological theories to be "true" and knowledge to be a chance of changing our fate, as Wilson (1980, 9, 196) does. The difference between consciousness and nature must be retained like that between the methods of biology and sociology.

82. Both are closely related.

Whoever demolishes the difference between empirical science and philosophy, that is, holds a materialistic philosophy, runs the risk of claiming that the methodological differences between physics and biology, between sociology and biology, between ethics and biology, and so on are only temporarily valid "emergency solutions" for the beginning stages of science. The final solution then dissolves the "higher" by the more basic forms of science. The plurality of sciences and the constant irreducibility of the "higher" levels of science to the lower levels (that investigate the basis of the higher levels and thus are seen as a necessary but not sufficient basis) are only secured if it is accepted that philosophical problems cannot be reduced to scientific ones. From this it follows for a sociology that does not want to abdicate in favor of sociobiology that it be open to a philosophical thematization of its approaches and consequences, and this implies thematizing its relation to its very subject matter.

83. The content of these scientific theoretical considerations of principle can also be attained if one observes the self-reflection of the sociologists as it is expressed in their large conventions. In Germany the "positivism debate" that began on the occasion of the convention in Tübingen in 1961 extended beyond its own subject matter (see Adorno 1987). The main opponents were, on the one side, K.R. Popper and K. Albert, and, on the other side, Th. W. Adorno and J. Habermas. The conflict consisted to a great extent in Popper and Albert positing an interpretation of sociological work

from the ideal of an objective, value-free understanding of structure, whereas Adorno and Habermas wanted to view sociology as an instrument for the analysis of the current dominating conditions and with respect to the amelioration of society, thus, very valued and taking a side. Irrespective of the sundry conceptions of society and science that were involved therein, the two sides could at least verbally agree by the end of the meeting that one could attempt to determine the kind and selection of objects of sociological research through the interests of the public welfare, that is, to demand such determination—but also that the development of sociological theories is to occur according to immanent, purely objective methodological principles (see Schulz 1972, 158–178).

84. During the Twentieth German Sociologist Convention in Bremen in 1980 the theory-practice relationship in sociological research came to the forefront once again, although in a different context. The sociologists had, in the meantime, obtained a very large share of the functions in interpreting existence in West German society: constitutive elements (mostly liberal) of sociological theories and terminology entered into the general language of educated people. At this point, especially conservative sociologists, such as H. Schelsky (1975) or Fr. Tenbruck (see Matthes 1982), objected to the improper scientizing of practical consciousness for actions that resulted from this and to the resulting key role of sociologists for the interpretation of life—a position of power easily misused. Again, the issue at hand is the problem of distorted communication, the problem of execution of power by an elitist group. Granted, it was not the future classless and repression-free society that was to function as an ideal picture anymore, but rather the memories of forms of society that prevailed in earlier times.

85. That leading sociologists of all persuasions immediately become philosophers when they attempt to become clearer about the orientation of their own scientific community is not surprising. Sociology (and the social sciences as

a whole) and social philosophy (along with the theory of social scientific knowledge) are open to one another and independent research directions.

The philosophy of the social refers especially to the following questions: To what extent do other individuals, to what extent society, belong to the constitution of the individual — and vice versa? Under which conditions can these relations, in principle and in concrete, be seen as successful? For our purposes the first complex of questions interests us most.

3. CRITICISM OF EXTREME POSITIONS

In order to clear up the question as to what extent the "you" and the "we" belong to the "I," one can look to an analysis and criticism of the model positions of individualism and collectivism. Both positions which offer a "smooth" solution to our speculative and practical problem can be traced back to J. J. Rousseau.

86. Individualism conceives of every form of human community (insofar as it is not purely natural as the family is) according to the model of a free agreement or contract between people who have power over themselves and have consented to other things in light of a common goal. Even where there is no explicit contract, one must interpret society as if it came to be through such a contract. For the existence and value of a society are secondary when compared with the existence and value of the individual. Thus, there is an ethical and ontological argument for individualism. Ontological: All reality is individual. Each individual has a prior substantial existence, whereas the existence of society is grounded in the relations among the individuals, and these relations themselves represent an unessential (= "accidental") category of being, and the weakest one as well. Ethical: The value of the person is the highest; every person has an inalienable right to liberty; no one has rights over the liberty of others (with the exception of provisionally and in the best

interest of the other, e.g., the rights of parents). Thus, the rights of others over my actions arise through my freely relinquishing some of them to others (generally in exchange for . . .).

87. Collectivism starts with the insight that a whole as such is not comprehensible from its parts if they are taken absolutely, that is, not as parts. Rather, the whole is prior to the parts. The basic model for this position is that of an ordered organism — one sometimes speaks of a social body, corporation, and so on. Once again there is an ontological and an ethical argument. Ontological: Whatever has its own formal laws has its own existence. Just as the formal laws cannot be derived from the form of the isolated individuals, the existence of the society cannot be derived from the existence of the individuals. On the other hand, individuals are comprehensible as elements of a society, so that the existence of the society has priority over that of the individual. The same is true from an ethical perspective. The common welfare is prior to individual goals. Only when a human being finds a comprehensive society for which he can sacrifice himself does he find personal fulfillment.

Both model theories claim unrelinquishable insights and concerns. We must mediate between the two so that the following becomes apparent: society and individuality are dialectically related to one another. Neither one is itself without the other. From this it follows: neither one is reducible to the other. This insight is to be developed in the following via a criticism of both of the one-sided models. That the emphasis of the criticism deals with the weaknesses of individualism is motivated by the inclination of our present Western society in this direction.

a) Criticism of Collectivism

88. In part the arguments that individualism uses for its thesis can be used against the collectivistic interpretation and restructuring of public affairs. Society never lies prior to its

own value and free decision such that it could subsist without free consensus and ground all rights in societal statutes. First, beyond all natural factors which can only ground the tendency to form social groups and not the groups themselves and beyond all force that will always only have a subsidiary function, the most important and indispensable constitutive factor of every society that is to be humane or at least function is the consent of the individuals to existence in this group and the free submission to its laws. The authorities must, therefore, attempt to gain and enable as great an identification of its members with their society as possible. For the agreement of the various individual wills in a common whole that corresponds to the needs of the particular human beings in its order—especially the social needs—constitutes the essential "substance" of every special society. The consent of the individuals is normally only given under the condition that certain basic rights of the individual are respected in this society and certain basic needs fulfilled. These basic rights lie prior to the judicial claims of the society and their official positions for the individual. In order to become valid law they must—in democratic societies at least—be formulated in the form of a law and passed by a legislative body.

However, these statutes have the character of an official recognition of a right that is preposited. What emerges clearly in its peculiarity in the realm of the state—under the title of basic rights or human rights—because it receives its contours in contrast to the posited rights—is true for smaller groups as well. Thus, education that is to raise a small child into an obedient citizen must not only confront the moods of the child with limits of commands and prohibitions (as well as the corresponding positive and negative "reinforcement") in its own interest, but it must do this in a manner in which the child is compelled to accept these limits not without any explanation but rather from a feeling of being loved. Educators should, therefore, not treat the child like an object of their possession but rather must respect it as the subject of original rights, that is, as a free being that must be taken as such so that it will become such. (That structures similar to those between individuals and societies are, or should be, present in the relationship of smaller communities to overarching social forms is a subject matter of social philosophy and not anthropology.)

b) Criticism of Individualism

89. Against the individualistic outlook and mode of existence found in contemporary societies it is not enough to point out that everywhere and at all times human beings have lived in social groups, although there have always been human beings who, freely or not, went into inner or outer exile. One must show, rather, that every society has a structure that cannot be reduced to the wills of the parties that have constituted the social contract. One must show that free individuals are mere individuals next to further groups yet to be constituted, but never simply individuals, that is, that every "I" stands in an essential relation to the "we" and "you."

90. The phenomenon of authority belongs to every form of human society. One or several members can make demands of other members that have their legitimacy in the membership of these individuals in the society. Thus, one can be reminded of certain imposed duties by other members who, by doing so, exercise a function of authority. Such functions of authority can be institutionalized in certain offices that are then occupied either for longer or shorter periods of time by members. It is not necessary, however, that they be institutionalized. A wife who reminds her husband of certain duties that he has as a husband is not speaking as Mary Jones, but rather as a representative of the ethical structure of marriage; she exercises authority. That she can exercise this function as one who is affected thereby and on this particular man is grounded in the contingent fact of her marriage contract. However, the both of them did not originate the social form of marriage; rather they took it over for themselves—

and not only because the institution was already there. If they had discovered it for the first time, they would have found themselves in a network of rights and duties (formulated externally) of which they would have gradually become aware and, thus, which need not expressly be made in order to be legitimate. One can object that these rights and duties were implied in the "I do" of the contract in which certain actions are mentioned and are, therefore, valid through it. This, however, only states that one is free to enter into a marriage or free not to do so. Why should the arbitrariness of marrying (this man) or not carry on into whether one should meet its expectations or not? Only because the marriage contract does not create duties but rather expresses its being taken over by you and me.

91. Perhaps, however, duties only arise if I freely relinquish portions of my rights to liberty that are principally and inalienably mine in order to receive corresponding portions of rights from others in society. What is certain is that factual claims of others over me do not yet constitute a duty for me, because otherwise one could not distinguish between legitimate and illegitimate demands. It is also certain that I relinquish a portion of my rights to time and money to others when I enter into a company, club, or marriage. What right must I have given up, however, so that others can pose the justified expectation of me to be friendly or compassionate to them and not to live as if I were the only inhabitant at the middle point of the world? I can only relinquish that toward which I stand in a possession relation. Additionally: A right that I can relinquish must belong to me in the first place, that is to me and not to another. In the concept of right the recognition of the other is already involved, even when I have or believe I have the right to this recognition. The right of property is a social phenomenon, not a presocial fact. That exclusivity, peculiar to property, must be recognized in order to be a right shows that sociality arises not from the exchange of property but rather vice versa: that all legitimate exclusivity of property recurs to a certain de-

velopment of the already-given social relation with respect
to the goods and services that can be utilized by everyone.
Finally, no one is an individual and then socializes oneself.
Rather, we grow up in a form of social relation from which
we can then transfer to other changing ones.

92. This last motive has been developed especially by developmental psychology. The human being becomes an independent center of consciousness and actions (to an ego)
in the course of physical maturation in which the mother
and father play (especially in the earlier stages) the indispensable role of a stable contact person (see Spitz 1967). The
child does not grow internally without becoming, through
verbal interaction, aware of the possibilities it is just beginning to develop. If it is not spoken to (in the sense that in
being spoken to certain processes of awareness are awakened
or approached), it does not become linguistic. By whom and
how a small human being is spoken to goes into its later life-
form as a persistent foundation: supportive or cumbersome,
but at any rate indelible. Thus, everyone carries in a sense
one's parents, siblings, and teachers around with one, and
in addition, since this is true for these people as well, an un-
foreseeable community of human beings out of the past—
although to an extent that generally diminishes with temporal proximity. That parents consciously and unconsciously
recommend their judgments and biases, their attitude and
lifestyle, for the child to imitate along with their love that
liberates their humanity—this fact binds the young human
being at the same time to a certain culture: as it is dominant in the family, the class, the country, the cultural region,
and so on. The growing out of the physical and psychic maternal womb into independence is, at the same time, a growing into new forms and qualities of social relations. "Being
directed from without" and "internal steering," just as "ego
identity" (in a psychological sense) in general, are unthink-
able without constant social mediation (E.H. Erikson
1956/57 and 1963).

93. Of course, one could reply, a human being is a social

being from its initial forms, no different than other primates. What is important, however, is that one liberates oneself from being solely directed by one's desires (or instincts) by learning to be led by rational and moral considerations (or autonomously), so that the actual development of a human being occurs within the nurturing of a social group to become an independent, ultimately irrevocably solitary individual, that is, in the "individuation" (C.G. Jung; see Jacobi 1967 and 1968, 107ff.). In the goal of one's personal development there stands the acquisition, only to be achieved by oneself, of an isolation that is intrinsic to the reflecting ego and dissolves all immediacy. Certainly there is an ultimate isolation that appears to be burdened upon every grown and growing up human being, and perhaps especially the members of contemporary Western culture. This isolation lies on a deeper anthropological level than the factual isolation and feeling of loneliness that arises because I am standing on the outskirts of social life, have been left by my mate, or am poor at making contact with other human beings due to some childhood trauma. This deeper isolation can become conscious in connection with such a separation experience, but it can also be hidden through dealing with that experience. Conversely, it can break out in times of great happiness or intense encounters. Its content is the tautology that is not necessarily obvious: I am I—that all identifications with other people are only detours with transient effects and no relief from the burden of having to be oneself.

94. The experience of being essentially "thrown back" upon oneself is related in two ways to the horizon of others: once, negatively insofar as the other proves to be foreign by pulling back from a lasting association through me, and again, positively insofar as the other becomes experienced as another, in his own existence. In such a manner this experience of limitation is related to the transition between two ways of living interpersonal relationships. "Proximally and for the most part"—taking up Heidegger's expression—we move in the first kind of relationship in which everyone

uses everyone as a mediation of his egocentric goals, at least to a certain degree. At the same time our self-relation is characterized by a lack of avoidance of a confrontation with the severity of the ego's loneliness. This primary egoism is never completely discarded; its secret basic thesis that I am the center of *the* world because I am the center of *my* world is never definitively refuted (actually it is not meaningful to speak of "refutation" in the realm of our directly practical beliefs). Nevertheless, egoism can be permeated more or less by the attitude of altruistic love that accepts the other's own existence and gives the other room for it. For — and this is decisive — I cannot enable myself to accept the "fact" that I am myself and have to be myself — a fact of which no one can relieve me. I cannot make plausible to myself that it is good that it is precisely myself who is there. I can receive that acknowledgment only from the affirmation of another. Individuation removes the protection that the identification with the collective represents for everyone. It makes one lonely. But not only the dependency on a partner grows in this manner, but also the openness for the other in his own being develops. The individuated self is essentially related to the other in this twofold manner. Thus, no argument can be made for individualism from the fact of the inevitability of the ego's existence. For individualism always conceives of the individual from his — external or internal — private property. However, the individuated self does not belong — following G. Marcel — to the sphere of having, but rather to that of being.

4. THE EGO AND THE OTHER

95. Seen objectively, a relation between me and another is a relation between two human beings, one-sided or reciprocal. I, too, can observe my relations in an objective-distanced way, but then I am thematizing it not as I experience it. If I do this, I use a personal pronoun "I," "he" ("she," "you,"

"we"), and so on. These do not function as names for a subset of persons in order to separate them from the whole set. Proper names or descriptions would do this just as easily. This function of separation belongs to the intention of the personal pronouns but does not constitute their meaning. Whoever uses the expressions "I," or "you," and so on not only makes clear about which object is being talked but also stands in a certain relation to the intended realities. Moreover, this relation is not to the object of a proposition (or statement), but rather to oneself as speaker and the other as hearer—and this in a manner that this standing-in-a-relation is not something like an afterthought to the separating identification. Rather, the converse is true insofar as every speech about an object—myself and yourself included—is spoken for you—without having to use the words "I" and "you." One could say that they are included in the speech act. That is correct with respect to the relation that lies in speaking and being spoken to, so much so that one can say that this relation is purely expressed if it is thematized nonverbally. For as soon as the words "I" and "you" occur expressly, the function of separation and, thus, objectification of the speaker into something spoken enters into the picture. The people spoken about can be counted: you and I and he and she and so on. In speaking and being spoken to, you and I are not two, but rather a unity of modes of personal relations, irreducible to each other. The personal pronouns primarily belong, not to the objective realm of speaking, but rather in the actuality of interpersonal speech acts that are conjugated according to the possible combinations of the personal pronouns (and/or the corresponding inflection suffixes).

96. Every reflection on the social situation of the human being must, therefore, note that the subjective quality of experience of the social relations, as they are expressed in the personal pronouns, is picked up into objective speech and not suppressed in favor of the idea of relation that can be applied equally well in physics and psychology. Of course,

one must formalize in the sciences, as well as in psychology. However, this must occur in such a manner that one can recognize oneself again in what is said. Otherwise it remains purely cognitive information and does not lead to a complete understanding of human beings. Psychology must speak objectively about a subjective topic, subjective subjectivity.

Until now we have spoken of the subject and subjectivity as an existing thing of a certain kind, that is, its mode of existence. We abstracted from the dialogue form in which subjectivity can only be present. We spoke from a neutral standpoint without considering that our talk is a subjective act of being, in each case from a certain, egocentrically oriented perspective to which "subjective" modes of experience and "subjective" interests belong.

a) Interpersonality and Intersubjectivity

97. We attempted, on the other hand, to bracket the merely subjective since our concern was the positing of a theory with objective validity that should, therefore, be true. The claim that such a theory must be evident for everyone belongs to its positing. Objectivity belongs to truth and intersubjectivity to objectivity. "Intersubjective" refers to the claim of validity that is made for statements. Every possible cognitive subject must be able to admit that this determinate statement is true. Why is this the case? Because truth is defined as that which is identical with itself, that is, everything that stands in contradiction to it is excluded (see the principle of noncontradiction). The truth is singular and has its determinateness in itself, prior to all individual acquisition of knowledge. Thus, the intersubjectivity of the validity of a statement is dependent upon the objectivity of this validity, that is, the truth of the statement, and naturally not vice versa. For an opinion being widely held does not make it true. Of course, the individual alone has difficulty proceeding past her own subjective opinions to the objective truth. One needs reciprocal correction, tutoring, and so on, but the basic capacity of each individual to arrive at a mini-

mal basis of knowledge on one's own is assumed. Otherwise I could not know whether the correction I was receiving was legitimate or not, and the blind would be teaching the blind about colors.

To the extent, however, that one is successful in coming to the objectivity of knowledge and in leaving behind the limitation of one's opinions through one's standpoint, one actualizes the idea of (finite) knowledge. This idea has an inner unity on which it is dependent as is the case for truth. To this inner unity of objectivity corresponds an inner unity of ideal subjectivity—not the always subjective subjects that vary through their different standpoints of interests, but rather the one "transcendental" subject in which all participate insofar as they have real objective knowledge. The "inter" in the expression "intersubjectivity" therefore means, not a relation between subjects, between you and me and them, rather that the difference of opinions in the different subjects about the same question is rescinded if these opinions are true. The various subjects then become, in a sense, one single subject to the extent they blossom in the "transcendental I"—whereby "transcendental" means here both "beyond experience" and "enabling experience."

98. How are intersubjectivity and interpersonality related if the latter expression stands for the fact of a reciprocal relation between you and me, and soon—formulated abstractly, between persons? In the idealistic tradition one attempted to understand the latter from the standpoint of the former, that is, to interpret the various egos with their conflicting opinions and intentions as a diminution and early stage of the unity of the one subject. It is clear that interpersonality is only possible if intersubjectivity is possible. For if human beings are not capable of coming to common beliefs that are tenable, or at least a manifold of undisputable points of view that converge toward one truth, human coexistence is not possible. Nevertheless, the thought of intersubjectivity offers too narrow a basis to build a theory of interpersonal relations upon it, and this for three reasons.

99. First, the qualitative and correlative differences of the

poles of relations that are represented by the—unspoken and spoken—personal pronouns cannot be dissolved into the homogeneous variety of the various egos or consciousnesses or even partial egos. The particular for-one-another, and not merely next-to-one-another, is lost in the process. The ego can be formed into a plural case ("the egos") but not the word "I."

Second, the adequate form of relation between epistemic subjects is the topic for discussion as whose goal the finding and accepting the common knowledge is already established. A related form of community is the cooperation of many people in producing a certain piece of work. The unity of the goal that is strived for by all is the reason for the community. It can occur, however, that although the goal is possessed by all, a relation between the subjects is not achieved, so that the goal, at least as a common one, cannot be actualized. Additionally, in the interpersonal realm one is not always concerned with actualizing a common goal: one is concerned with taming and seducing, ruling and reverence, manipulation and a feeling of community, threatening and a lack of interest, the gift and the taking of life. Human beings play *with* one another, not just together.

Third, in the horizon of intersubjectivity, feelings, interests, previous histories, and dreams only play the role of agitating factors that threaten oppression-free communication, that is, the unification of the subjects to one subject— at any rate, they have no constitutive role. However, they are the material from which interpersonal relations are made— also, for example, conversation (that is not to be seen as its special form, discussion).

b) The Other

100. The observer distinguishes one from another; there are two. The one differs from the other just as the other differs from the one. Either one can be taken as the first or the second. Conversely, I refer to you or to another person and posit

therewith the distinction between you and me or her that one can formalize as the distinction-in-reference from oneself and the other. This relation has a certain direction, not to be reversed in the portrayal, and grants the privilege to the one pole as the first one (see No. 28). My self-relation is essentially different than that to another, and this on its most basic level, irrespective of all modifications of the whole relation between both relations that constitute "my" comprehensive, subjective being (see No. 29 and No. 190; No. 193ff.).

101. What is the peculiarity of my primary self-relation, my I-existence? I am acquainted with myself. I experience myself and my world, in a sense, from "within," from the midpoint. This state of affairs coincides very well with the fact that I can know very little about who I really am, or that I can be (act) foreign to myself sometimes. For the egoistic being-at-another is something totally different than theoretical knowledge, and the intimacy that belongs to the ego establishes the possibility that I not know myself anymore. In contrast to this egoistic constitution through which my existence and my world are constantly given to me internally, I encounter the other from outside, embodied in a body and thus accessible, yet hidden. The other's behavior spells out parts of his thoughts, attitudes, and so on, but just a part and occasionally only partially. Different from what Behaviorism would like, the inner realm cannot be fully translated into behavior, even less so that it becomes clear. Not merely because the other can consciously hide her feelings and intentions or even mislead others, but also because the bodily appearance expresses the character and basic attitude of a human being in a way that can be crossed with other features (beauty/ugliness, sickness, hereditary form, etc.). Especially, however, I encounter the other as Other, who has an ego but is not myself.

102. The same asymmetry as regards the relationship to myself and to the other as it is shown in the mode of givenness, of consciousness, is found again in the mode of evalua-

tion, of love. I am the closest and most important and loved person—at any rate first and yet for the most part. The world is initially my world: whatever is important to me carries weight in this world. My opinions, preferences, and so on appear to me as normal and natural simply because they are mine. How do I initially experience the other, his opinions and feelings and intentions? As a threat and/or a fulfillment of myself? My tendency will, therefore, be to colonize or at least neutralize the other: to bring the other to do good things for me, not to convict me, not to despise, cheat, use me, and so on. If I am not successful, the possibility remains of making my vulnerability (poverty, incapacity, etc.) bearable through identification with the other. I participate respectfully in the power of "my General," in the beauty of "my lover," in the intelligence of a Nobel Prize Winner, my acquaintances, "my Nobel Prize Winner." If that is successful, the fear remains that the tamed other could stop being "mine" and break out in his otherness that is his original mode of existence. A different fear lies yet deeper, although it also has a sanguine side: the fear that my colonization could succeed too well. For then I would be powerful and certain, but this is not my only concern: rather I want to be freely accepted by the other, not forced or with reserves. In order to achieve this, I must free her from the chains of my judgments, through which I have come to terms with her, so that she can have the independence of her own initiatives; I must give her the space of trust in which she can come out of her shell. In order for me to be able to do this, however, I must have some trust to which, given the risks involved, courage and intelligence belong.

103. The other lives in such an ego-perspective as well as from the organization of his consciousness and his motivations. In his perspective I am the other. This, too, plays an important role for the way in which I encounter the other: what I know or believe about my position in the other's consciousness, judgment, and life. The constant back and forth of such reciprocal dynamic perspectives of one self to an-

other constitutes interpersonal life. It must fail or at least limit itself to the level of cooperation, exchange of things and services (which is a form of failure too!) as long as it is dominated by the attitude that experiences the other as an other-for-me, as the negation of my primary egocentric — that is, as merely "the other" characterized by nothing other than the fact that the other is distinct from me. In lone reflection, in which I am alone with myself, anyone who has or could exchange "you" with me has become an "other."

104. As soon as I experience the free donation of the other who enters into her ownness from otherness, in such a way that my ownness affirms "It is good that you are here!" I discover that my existence and the force of my self-affirmation are liberated and develop — that I essentially belonged to the other so that she can give to me — but not so that I can take myself away from her again in order to belong only to myself. Thus, I discover at the same time that the other belongs to me as well, so that I am capable of contributing to the acquisition of the other through my affection for the other. If this acquisition meets the most inner self, the affection must be selfless — leaving the other in his own existence and hiddenness. All pain that flows from the lack of or broken relationships and all happiness that blossoms out of successful relationships are founded in the fact that no ego can belong only to itself.

The comparison of the self-relation with the property relationship has played a dominant role in philosophy and in social life (to which personal life belongs) since the beginning of the modern period. I-ness and privacy have been interchangeable concepts to a large extent — the Other has become not only an existential problem but, as regards comprehension, also a philosophical problem in principle. We shall deal with this aspect of the topic "I and Others" in the chapter on consciousness (No. 187–190).

III. Historicity

105. In the course of anthropological reflection one comes across the topic "historicity" twice. First, historicity arises as a disrupting factor when we attempt to postulate a concept of humanity that is valid for all of time: the manifestations of human beings during the course of time are too diverse and our thought is too closely tied up with our historical situation. (We have already discussed this problem in No. 40–43). Second, it belongs to the specifically human act of existence to be situated in the present through a certain relation to the future and the past. The human being is a historically living organism. We want to address this fact in the following. We start with a reflection on the historicity of historical writing and grope forward from the idea of objective time to that of subjective time and, finally, arrive at a concept of historicity.

1. THE HISTORICITY OF HISTORICAL WRITING

106. History (the science of the researching and portrayal of history) is, as every science is, bound to the ideal of objectivity. History reports "how it really was" (Ranke) as opposed to legends that mix truth with falsehood or even fairy tales to which one enjoys listening but does not believe. If this is the case, why must history be written anew in every generation? Does not the status of knowledge imply knowledge forever?

107. Several reasons why the writing of history must start time and time again can easily coincide with the ideal of timeless objectivity of knowledge: new sources are discovered (an archive is found, a scroll is decoded, new techniques of dating are discovered, etc.), premature conclusions from a source that has not changed can be uncovered, previously unresearched epochs or neglected parts of history can be researched and the knowledge thus gained in this manner can be synthesized with what is already possessed. There are yet more reasons to which Jakob Burckhardt points when he writes: "The sources . . . are inexhaustible so that one has to read the books, exploited a thousand times before, because they give the reader and each century a special countenance. . . . It is possible that in Thucydides, for example, lies a fact of the first order that will not be noticed until a hundred years from now. . . . This is not a mishap, rather just a consequence of the constant lively business" (*Worldly Observations, Collected Works* IV, 15). The pictures of the past that replace one another are the product of an interpretation of sources from approaches that replace one another and result from the problems and line of questions of the particular presence of the researcher and the corresponding surroundings. That in previous times the detailed portrayal of the great battles was taken to be as important as the investigation of the structure of the economy and the life conditions of the great mass of population in history—that apparently depends upon the changed political structure of the society in which the historians live and for which they write.

108. The change in the historical protrayal reflects a change in the way one understands, finds difficult or unacceptable one's present time. Of course, the previous modes of interpretation remain to some extent intact since they are not refuted, rather merely discarded. Thus, one can speak of progress in historical knowledge. This progress is, however, different from that in physics, where Einstein's relativity theory not only discarded Newton's classic mechanical physics but rather envelops it into itself as a special case. The

historian cannot be this just. Because her object is not the hierarchy of structural laws, but rather the colored, intertwined concrete occurrences that can only seldom be interpreted as abstract functional laws and typical structures, that—as factors economic, political, sociological, psychological, and so on—permeate one another pluralistically, she must, in thematizing one topic or point of view, let many other topics or points of view fade into the dimness of the background. The most objective, self-critical researcher apprehends this structural "injustice." Even this is an ideal picture. For the human world of the past always stands in an inner connection with the human world of the present, whether it be continuous or analogous. Due to this aspect identifications and dislikes are carried over from the present into the recalled past, just as one, for example, can see in the portrayal of the history of the German command in German and Polish history books of today and yesterday. Whether intended by historians or not, to a greater or lesser extent every historical work will prove to be an ideological exaggeration or the passionate biases of a class, a period, or an individual. Even the attempt of a conscious, self-critical ascetic writing of history, even if it succeeds, will be influenced by the time's ideology against which the researcher fights.

109. What makes the past comprehensible and interesting for us is that it is always about us: about our people, our religion, the constant human condition in all its diversity. Even what is completely different, the far off, can interest us because it is the contrast to what we are acquainted with, the excluded (yet still conceivable) possibility, the beginning of our present time, and so on. Without this interest that radiates out into the various problems of life no one would bother with history. Thus, the interest in the past results from a fundamental interest in coming to terms with and the fulfillment of the present—because this is essentially a result of the past. To what extent and in what manner the thematization of the past belongs to coming to terms with

the present varies extensively: in epochs, classes, and individuals. The need for the past in a ruling house of nobility or for a citizen who can identify with his city is much greater than for a small farmer—for a Christian more than for an anthroposopher—since the nineteenth century much greater than previously. The extent and weight of the past and history are determined by the particular situation in the present. On the one hand, history is an attempt to represent the objective, past reality; on the other hand, the form in which a culture "accounts for itself" (J. Huizinga, *Im Banne der Geschichte (In the Power of History),* Amsterdam 1942, 104).

2. THE IDEA OF OBJECTIVE TIME AND THE TEMPORALITY OF THE SUBJECTIVE ACT OF SELF-EXISTENCE

110. The scientific research and portrayal of the past is a way of coming to terms with the historically transmitted present that is open toward the future. History is possible and—to a certain, historical extent—necessary through the historicity of the human act of existence, individually and collectively (of families, peoples, etc.).

We become aware of the past by connecting past events with one another on the background of an idea of the objective passage of time, as earlier and later, as a cause and an effect and, once again, as a cause. The basic structure of this objective time is given to us by physics, or, more precisely, astronomy: the sequence of years, months, and days. The homogeneous medium of this natural time crisscrosses a network of divisions that is already determined. A certain event is taken as basic for a reference point of dating (for years, something like Christ's birth or Mohammed's flight; for the counting of days, the fixing of a New Year's day, a monthly or weekly division, a calendar, etc.). Additionally, there are names for smaller or larger epochs that, on the one hand, serve to classify single events and divide the entirety of world history and, on the other hand, license particular national histories, events, and periods and, thus, indirectly suggest a certain way of understanding oneself. The large epochal divisions Ancient–Middle Ages–Modern lie on this level, the ordering of world history using Mediterranean European history, with its descriptions of periods of time such as "absolutistic," "feudal," and such as a guiding thread. Despite all the structuring of content that distinguishes historical time from natural time, historical time always remains founded in natural time, the irreversible sequence of uniform movement. In the following it is to be shown that this idea of time to which the historian refers is only possible due to a more primitive mode of temporality that is closely connected to the subject-character of the human being who can also be an historian.

111. Time is doubtless the unity of past, present, and future. This claim can be understood in three different, fundamental meanings.

In the first meaning the statement means approximately: time is the totality of all moments past, present, and future. This totality is the unity of an idea: the past times are reawakened out of their not-any-more by memories and, thus, brought to the present in their past; the future times are brought out of the not-yet through anticipation and, thus, brought to the present; and both rows are synthesized with the present to a single time. The present is, however, the now for the subject that is remembering, anticipating, and paying attention to something. This means two things. On the one hand, there is the now, the present from which both of the contrary dimensions of the past and future time diverge, each the acted present of a subject. Past, future, and present are meaningless expressions without the genitive subjective (Lat. *Genitivus subiectivus*). On the other hand, there is obviously a correlation between past and memory, future and anticipation, present and attention. As Augustine has said (*Confessions* XI, 14 ff.), past and future, even present, can only *be* for a being that is capable of remembering, anticipating, and paying attention. The clarification of what memory and so on are in their reciprocal unity leads to an elucidation of time. Seen factually, time is certainly not the product of the acts of the subject; it simply cannot "be" without the subject.

112. *How* are the future, past, and present here? In anticipation, remembering and attentively noting. The future becomes present in anticipatory expectation which can occur in two ways: either in the form of a closed process or in the form of a presently occurring process: in the first case the visualization of the future uses the form of the past; in the second case, the form of presence. The form of the past uses the form of the presence insofar as memory represents the past as a present event. Thus, our question concentrates on an investigation of what constitutes the presence of an event. Let's take the example of a melody. In order to hear a melody as such, I must grasp the individual tones as elements of a whole, and these as a rhythmic, tonal, and other ordered manifold. Viewed toward the momentary tones, that means: they can only be perceived in their specific "value" if the previously rung and presently ringing parts of the melody are retained just as the parts that may be approaching are already expected. Listening, retaining, and expecting affect each other reciprocally. In this manner the whole melody, a closed event that only has presence in the passing through of its parts, is built up. The totality of a temporal event is nothing that is temporal in the sense that it is reducible to the individual present or piecing together of individual "presents." The presence of the individual ringing tones is only one moment in the emergence of the presence of the melody, in the transition from anticipation to fulfillment, from partial fulfillment to anticipation.

Retention and expectation, connected with the actual recording of an event, as the correlates to a more primitive mode of past and future, support the memory of a completed story and the anticipation of a specific event. The memory (and what that anticipated) has an objective presence, whereas the retained and expected, together with the present that both combines and separates them, leads to an objective presence.

113. We can now move from the second meaning of time as the unity of retained past, expected future, and accepted present to the third. Time in the second meaning is the inner form of experience that proceeds objectively in front of my summarizing, inner eye; it belongs in the realm of objective consciousness (see No. 162). Is the form of time for an objective portrayal of temporal events necessarily and always the inner temporality of the temporal events? (See the difference between subjective and objective unity in No. 27!) In other words, there is a difference between the time that belongs to objectively visualized processes and the time that belongs to the subjective occurrence of the visualization itself — and to the life of the subject as it is primitively given in self-awareness. Naturally, we can picture our life objectively by orienting ourselves with the life forms of others; I would then be sitting, in a sense, in an audience in front of a stage on which my own life is played like a theatrical work: simplified into the unity of a single (hi-)story with a beginning, middle, and end. However, I do not merely take over the formal standpoint from which others grasp my life. The others must supplement the picture of my life where I have forgotten or was never fully aware of it.

However, how am I to experience life in its temporality while I am living it and not just picturing it? One does not want to claim that time is merely a form of representation and not of life as well, although time as the form of representation and time as the form of life have different structures. To what extent do I live time, my time? Insofar as I am certain that I am constantly confronted with possibilities that extend beyond what is already factually occurring. Thus, I experience the future. Insofar as I know that I am not starting at point zero, rather was already there in a certain way, through which certain possibilities are given and others excluded before I freely decide on them, that is, that I am determined by the necessity of the past. I actualize the present insofar as I grasp the possibilities in which the unused fullness of the past approaches me. The past, summed up for its result, is present in the consciousness of agency without it being objectively remembered. It has its own present as the limiting ground for new things; this present is, thus, incomplete and closer to being merely a moment in the present in the normal sense. The future is present, not as the anticipated present or past, but rather as the approach of possibilities that are striving for realization. The time of action that dynamically underlies the time of the objectively perceivable can be interpreted as the dialectic unity of real possibility (future), necessity (past), and factuality (present), as the connection between the three ontological modalities. The concern is the unity of contraries, but contraries that belong together such that each one is only what it is in virtue of its contrast to the others. That is true formally for the future, past, and present as such. It is true in concrete cases as well. Which possibilities can be mine is determined by my past; whatever the content of my past is is determined by the future possibilities of further development or restructuring; and both of these narrow down to the eye of the needle of the present decision and is then decided, creating a new constellation of difference between past and future.

The purely dialectic relation of past, future, and present is the most inner structure of time and act of subjective mode of existence. Naturally, there are as few "purely" free decisions (see No. 199), dissolved from any concrete modes of possibility, necessity, and factuality, as there is time in its primitiveness. Time must always be, even if to differing extents, the time of running processes — the time with which we calculate and we can order by counting. Thus, the basis is laid for the concept of historicity.

3. HISTORICITY

114. The expression "historicity" is used in two different fields of application. It can denote a basic constitution of human beings and their world *in general* or the charac-

teristic of a *specific* culture. In the first case the concern is an anthropological concept; in the second case, a culturological one (sociological, humanities). We shall deal with the latter only in a short appendix (b), and the anthropological issue in more detail (a).

a) Dialectic of Historicity

115. We always read the general structure of something off examples that worked best—at the same time, or perhaps even more, those which were defective and not successful —which point toward the primitive totality of the structure. This is how we proceeded in the last two chapters, and this is how we will proceed here. The expression "historicity of human existence" means the fact that each individual human being not only has a past behind him and a future in front of him but also has developed a relationship which determines how he has his past "behind him," his future "in front of him," and his present "in him." This relationship consists in perceptions, values, and decisions, more or less conscious, more or less free. It refers to the individual's life story as well as the history of the community with which the human—to a greater or lesser extent—identifies, making the past and future his past and future.

116. "We are living in the present" (Straus 1956, 417)— not in the timeless present of representations of processes or stories that are in the present perfect tense, rather in the now that comes and goes. This present cannot be represented as long as it is present; it is essentially an act. This act comprehends a certain, representative possession of the future and past. This possession can mishap on the side of the future as well as on the side of the past so that it never comes to a complete present. Two cases can be distinguished: the dissolution of the lived present into the lived representation of lived past or future (No. 117–118) or the hindrance of lived present through the (partial) loss of past or future (No. 120–121).

117. One can put oneself into past conditions and actions as if one lived in them now; one lives experienced events once more and gets a feel for what the others experienced. Similarly, one can project oneself into future experiences, in pleasure or achievement as well as threats or defeats that are anticipated playfully. All of this is meaningful as long as it remains positively related to the present situation. It can take place, however, such that it replaces the present situation. One does not live in the present but rather in the past or in the future because one only finds life worthwhile there. This results in a loss of reality for all three temporal modes; reality becomes a dream. For the present is now the present of one who is absent, and that, as an event fixed in itself, has no reference to the lived present—except for replacing it. The future does not revive the present but rather covers it up by becoming the apparent present. The past, also an apparent present, suffocates the present instead of leading up to it. Thus, life in memories of anticipations proves to be a life as a replacement-present if it becomes the dominating life form.

118. Conversely, it is apparent that what belongs to life in the present suffices without fleeing forward or backward: the perception and acceptance of the momentarily given possibility of production, entering into relations and pleasure. These possibilities are different now than tomorrow or yesterday. Certain possible courses of action remain for a long time, whereas others, often the most important and valuable, have their hour in which they come and go, are taken up or let pass by. Time, as the medium of action and life, is not a continuous, homogeneous manifold of places. Whoever wants to master life must learn to do only what is appropriate at the time. For the fortunate moment or the decisive hour that occurs is such with respect to a value about which I must already have decided in order to be able to recognize the fortunate opportunity, the due measure — and after critical consideration, not simply for reasons of conformity. That does not exclude but rather includes the fact

that the decision for a value that has a validity for various situations is not completed until it finds a concrete situation in which its realization is believed possible. Not until then does the value shine forth in its concreteness as benevolent, binding, and so on. All of this has nothing to do with opportunism or historically foreign "principled" thought that assumes the fiction of repeated identical situations of action.

119. The true present, as the time of action, is determined not only by being different from the past and future insofar as these are represented presents but also by the past and future permeating it in a sense. For all action—this word is to be taken in a wide sense—is the transgression of what has existed until now into something new and is, thus, a new determination of meaning for the past. This brings us to the second aspect which we characterized as the hindrance of lived present by the (partial) loss of past or future.

120. The expression "loss of past" does not refer to the fact that someone (or a group) has had a short or simple past, free of astonishing peculiarities, but rather the phenomenon that one has one's past present in a manner such that it hinders or prevents true present. The "volume" of the present of a human being or group that cannot find a positive relationship to its past is strangely thin. The past is there in any case and cannot be discarded; it, gathered together into a result, constitutes the starting point from which one is to continue or from which one can change things and start anew. It can, however, be there such that it is constantly posited in place of the present, because in a sense it cannot recede similar to the unliberated dead spirits of tribal superstition. That is the case for compulsive repetition, for the burden of an unforgiven guilt and for depression due to a loss that has not been mourned. Such a past cannot be fruitful for the present but rather lies as a heavy stone on top of the present. It can only be set free into the past if one remembers it expressly, if one lets the unfortunate event, against all resistance, into one's awareness and provides it a new place by accepting the event into one's past.

Where there had previously been holes, gaps, and empty periods in one's memories of one's life and its completeness, there arises a greater integrity and continuity. How difficult, but also how necessary, such a positive relationship is to the past can be shown by the present of those human beings and peoples (e.g., especially the Germans) that are determined by the bracketing of essential parts of their history. However, a past that is not in need of recovery cannot simply be put into the file cabinet. Memories of the past are essential for learning from experience, especially in those realms of learning that are hardly touched by the operation of mediation through cognitive learning. Remembering is also important in the sense of relativizing one's present viewpoint, ideals, habits, and, thus, for the liberation of productive fantasy that plans the future. It is also important for the meditative acquiring of experiences that, in the hustle and bustle of the impressions, could only be enjoyed and respected to a limited extent. Due to such reflection thankfulness increases — a feeling that enables one as few other experiences do to being present and open for the future. All of what we have said about the effects of one's relation to the past on one's relation to the present is, of course, also true for one's relation to the future.

121. It stands exactly reversed for the consequences that accompany the loss of the future: past and present are affected. If someone does not expect anything else from life, then he will have so little energy that he will be lived more than he himself will live. The past can easily become an asylum into which he projects himself; at any rate, the past will not be experienced as fruitful ground for today and tomorrow. Whoever does not trust in a far-reaching continuity of the future with the past will not have the courage to enter into a larger project or community. For whomever the future constantly brings forth the same old thing and cannot bring about anything new, that one will hold strongly to tradition more than the normative in the practical realm and to the (apparent) regularity in everything in the theoretical

realm. If no other future is offered than that of being the son, heir, or student of a great elder, for such a person the future will be a nightmare. If one (half unconsciously) imagines that an infinite sequence of new, constantly repeating possibilities lies ahead, then what is necessary will be put off and the available will slip away. If one realizes that one day there will be no more future, then one appreciates the value of available time and will be less tempted to escape an unacceptable past into an ideal future.

122. Human beings and every human community are, therefore, arranged in a dialectical relationship between, on the one hand, a certain, invariable past that is, nevertheless, formable by the future and, on the other hand, a malleable future that is not yet available, but arranged such that they can and must carry out this relation in a creative way (see Müller-Halder 1971, 99). More comprehensive than our capacity to arrange is the fact that we have been arranged. It is true that we can take a stand even on this fact, but only in the sense of either attempting to order oneself into it or escaping into one of the other portrayed modes, which, however, can only be unreal. (See No. 235 to 237.) The end of our life which we cannot escape and the beginning of our life in which we simply find ourselves are facts whose control does and cannot lie in our power, either theoretically or practically. Although science attempts to banish the uncertainty of the future through predictions and planning, this can only succeed, in principle, to a limited degree. Similarly, we attempt to figure out the origin and meaning of tradition via the methods of science so that we are not indebted to some dark, unfathomable power, but this dissolution of power also quickly reaches its limits. The rational reconstruction of traditional customs and points of view quite often do not succeed, although we cannot be sure that the tradition does not have any or any more meaning which would allow us to discard it in good conscience. Even where rational reconstruction appears to be succeeding, the same uncertainty remains, namely, whether the tradition has other

possible interpretations and assumptions. Nonetheless, one can only creatively propagate what one can understand. The reference to the prominence of the traditional process over a self-critical and autonomous adaptation process can warn of too high a rating of the present reconstruction possibilities but should not be understood as a defense of mere acceptance and mediation.

b) The Historicity of Historicity

123. Historicity as such belongs to the characteristics of human existence of all times and cultures. The "how" of its act of existence, however, in its epoch-making, national and individual influence is very variable; it itself has a (or many) history(ies).

The historian and cultural anthropologist can investigate the different cultures in order to determine what degree of historical influence and awareness is present; one then finds more or less or even nothing at all as far as historicity is involved (see Homann 1974). The comparison can refer to different cultures or to different stages of one and the same culture.

124. In the first respect, Hegel, for example, denies that the tribes of black Africa have historicity at all because they have no concept of objective laws of nature and freedom and, thus, no state that stands above the volition of the individuals, whereas the development of the state is necessary for the meaning of history understood as progress (*Lectures on the Philosophy of World History* 128f.). In a different way Eliade calls primitive societies ahistorical insofar as these revolt against the concrete historical time and interpret all events as repetitions of the archetypical events in the beginning (1966,7).

125. In the second respect, many authors (e.g., Müller 1976, 16–18) speak of the prehistoric, historic, and post-historic epochs of a culture, not with respect to available sources or the declaration of a certain, especially outstand-

ing epoch to the center of the historical *portrayal,* but rather
with respect to the inner movement of life itself. If the concern in prehistorical times is the securing of biological survival and in posthistorical times more the preservation of
the satisfaction of the needs of a mass society, then history
is the battle for the sensual structuring of the contact of human beings to each other, to their divine origin and goal,
and to their own tradition.

126. Regardless of the correctness and fruitfulness of these
theories that need not concern us here, it becomes clear that
the so-called ahistorical mode of existence and culture is a
special modification of the formal, anthropological historicity, not its absence. For it is not at all simply a "natural"
animal-like standing in time, but rather the development of
a very special relationship to the extension into the dimensions of one's own past or future. The predicates "historical" or "ahistorical" are arranged with respect to a very *specific way* of standing in history, namely, such that history
is seen as the time of self-production via progressive (continuous or recurring anew) structuring of the world and formation of society. Seen anthropologically, the most pregnant
historical times as well as ahistorical times are modes of historicity—although this is not tantamount to the claim that
they must be intended in the same sense. For the historical
cultures have formed the concept of formal historicity so that
it is a product of history.

IV. Bodiliness

127. The leading concept that determines the line of our interpretation of anthropological phenomena is the concept of subjectivity: the act of a self-relation that is, at the same time, a relation to another. As long as this other is another human being or another thing, it has its own set contours through which it can be identified by an outside observer as something different than me. However, there is something for me which stands neither clearly on the side of the other nor clearly on the side of the self: it is my body. To interpret the phenomenon of bodiliness constitutes a decisive part of the interpretation of subjectivity.

1. A PRELIMINARY CONCEPT OF BODILINESS TAKEN FROM LANGUAGE

128. As soon as we talk about the body outside of the living context, the idea of a living puppet comes to mind. In order to push back this—as we shall see—distorted idea to make room for the reality of bodiliness, it is helpful to steer the analysis in the right direction with a preliminary concept. We can get this direction from three short considerations taken from the realm of language. We shall thematize, in this order, (a) the degree of body metaphors in language, (b) the bodily constitution of language itself, and, finally, (c) the methodological problematic of the hiddenness of bodiliness.

a) The Body Metaphors in Language

129. Probably in all, but certainly in our European, languages there are innumerable words whose basic meanings designate parts of the body or bodily modes of behavior but beyond that also serve to refer to all possible kinds of realities, functions, and modes of existence. One need only think, for example in English, of words like acting, standing, running, stretching, present, heart, taste, and so on, along with their related forms and composites (as an example we can take the word standing: understanding, outstanding, upstanding, etc.). The internal supplementation of the ambiguity of these expressions is the ambiguity of their corresponding expressions: just as no one can, literally, stand where there is no ground, the same is true metaphorically. Thus, words like "air," "room," "house," "nutritious," "distanced," and so on belong to the bodily metaphors. Several derivative words belong in this group as well: for example, chef (French: the head) or chapter (Latin: *caput:* head). In such cases the bodily meaning is covered up, as it is for a large part of our corresponding English expressions, that is, our way of using them. Still, one does not only have the impression that greater respect for the bodily primitive meanings can be very advantageous for the terseness of the language derived from them. The fact of the ambiguity of our expressions remains especially questionable. There must have been some reason for making a word that initially indicates sensual bodily aspects a designator for completely separate things and activities. In principle: there must be some reason for the fact that such a carry over (Greek: *meta-phorà*) of the meaning from one level of meaning to the other could and can take place. The feeling one has when losing the ground from underneath one's feet, in an existential sense, is similar to the feeling when this happens literally during a hike. If one must "swallow" too many demands, humiliations, and such that are "difficult to digest," then one's "stomach" may be turned by one's condition and become sick just as someone

who has eaten too many rich meals. The reason for this is that the bodily-psychic and psychic-mental functional realms are interwoven such that no one can close oneself off without running into—at least partially—the other. The immanent regularities of the physiological, psychical, and mental orders are of basically different kinds, but it is not only a structural analogy that exists between them but also a reciprocal translatability of modes of existence of the one order into the other that can be witnessed by language, so that, on the one hand, the metaphorical use of the word and act of life do not survive without the "literal" one and, on the other hand, the complete contents of the one are developed in the other. For this reason there must be a unity underlying these differences.

b) The Bodily Constitution of Language

130. Although meaning and phonetic sequence are completely different, we find them, while reflecting on language, in a primitive amalgamation such that differences on the side of the meanings correspond to differences on the side of the meaning-carriers (the phonemes). The meaning-carriers (the linguistic signs) and the meanings (the linguistically meant) are related, as de Saussure liked to say, as the front and back side of the same leaf. If one cuts the one side, the other side is cut along with it. This is true, as we have already seen, not for any arbitrary phonetic configurations, but only for those that belong to a language, as phonemes, morphemes, and such. The "leaf" is thus the language itself. In it phonetic expression and meaning do not have separate existences but rather have the mode of existence of reciprocating principles of a peculiar, insoluble phenomenon. That the comparison with the unity of body and soul—and, correspondingly, talk about the spirit of a language—comes to mind is, once again, probably not a coincidence. The understanding of the peculiarity of language (contrasted with both of its elements isolated) most often coincides with the under-

standing of the inscrutability of the body (contrasted with both of its elements isolated). The same is true for disinterest and lack of understanding. Examples, on the one hand, are Aristotle, Hamann, and Heidegger and, on the other hand, Plato, Kant, and Husserl. A whole theory of bodiliness can be developed from an analysis of language (see Bruaire 1968).

c) To What Extent Is the Body a Phenomenon?

132. A body can be observed and discussed: as large or small, as pretty or ugly, as sick or healthy. Seen in this manner, it is a phenomenon like other objective, aesthetic, or organic phenomena, but its peculiarity as a body remains blinded or tacitly presumed. How can the body be a phenomenon as body? The Zürich psychiatrist M. Boss points out a paradox here: "Characteristically human existence . . . means to let one be taken in by the encounter 'with body and soul' and to answer this reception correspondingly with word and deed. In such a truly human behavior the body as body is not there any more for the agent" (1971, 273). The body becomes a phenomenon for the observer to the extent that she loses her bodiliness. As long as she is a body, thus, not yet turned into a "physical object" according to the paradigmata of the natural sciences (for the distinction between body/physical object see Scheler 1913/16, 409ff.), its mode of givenness is indirect. This is not merely true for the self-experience of the bodily acting human being but also for the body of the person I am encountering. For I encounter *someone* who is there bodily (whose body is, thus, there too). In both cases the body stands in a kind of copresence. Of course, this copresence can swing around at any moment into—even if only fleetingly—a thematic presence, but it contains a recommitment to the original mode of experience. This thematic presence is the (necessary, but not sufficient) basis for the development of the scientific research of the body. The transparency and the transiency of the one mode

of presence into the other or of seclusion into the present
and vice versa belong to the simple concept of body.

2. THE REDUCTION OF THE BODY TO
A PHYSICAL OBJECT

133. In normal linguistic use there is no set limit in meaning between the expressions "body" and "physical object."
If one is made here, then it is in reaction to the terminology
of stereometrics and physics in which the word "body" is
set to designate a part of space bordered by straight or curved
surfaces or a certain mass with a constant or changing shape.
This concept of body has a different, more narrow meaning
than does the normal linguistic word "body." Nonetheless,
body can be viewed as a special case of physical objects. In
this manner it is the object of the (structurally dependent)
sciences of stereometrics, physics, and physiology. If one views
as the essence of natural appearances whatever invariant
structure can be found in them, one will try to interpret the
higher sciences as subclasses of the basic sciences and, correspondingly, the higher-leveled phenomena as complex connections of simple structures.

134. Thinking in these tracks, Descartes (e.g., in his *Principia* I, 53; II, 4.9) determined the essence of sense appearances as whatever can be made geometrical: namely—
according to his conception—extension and movement. (That
Leibniz soon added force to these determinations does not
imply any decisive changes in the frame of reference that lies
in its being made mathematical.) Thus, the diversity of the
colors, the variety of the smells, and the richness of tactile
qualities are all eliminated from the realm of true being. For
these only enter into the consciousness of a sensual being
organized in a specific manner. In the same vein, the teleological categories are to be viewed as something that is projected onto the real things. These, in their complexity, are
nothing other than functional wholes of movable extended

things; they are machines. The bodies of animals and human beings are also to be viewed as such machines.

Granted, there is also the faculty of understanding that questions, on the one hand, the appearances critically as to their underlying existence and, on the other hand, its own opinions self-critically as to their truth and certainty—sure of itself in all of its activities and standards, independent of all factual circumstances—that are only to be claimed after critical scrutiny. The order of the simple and the self-critical consciousness that reassures itself and the order of structured extension in the realm of sensual matter are fundamentally different. In themselves neither one points toward the other, despite being so intimately interwoven in our own existence, just as an undeniable and mysterious self-experience bears witness to: hunger, for example, is a conscious fact and a state of the body-machine at the same time.

135. If the modes of finite existence have exhaustively been listed with the twofold division of understanding (*res cogitans*) and mechanics (*res extensa*), then the question naturally arises, how it is possible that both of them, while capable of neither a matter-form relationship nor interaction, can occur in human experience as a true unity prior to analysis? Descartes did not ask this question. He posits normal experience as a third kind of consciousness in addition to the understanding's knowledge of geometry and physics and the faculty of reason's knowledge of philosophy without, however, also admitting a third kind of being at the same time.

His successors were not content with this ontological incompleteness. Initially attempts were undertaken, on the basis of dualism, to arrive at an understanding of the unity of body and spirit by having the *res cogitans* and the *res extensa* arise out of a common ground. This common ground was, not the existence of human beings, but rather either the free creation of God (Occasionalism) or nature that brings forth all things (Spinozaism).

136. The Occasionalists had God bring forth correspond-

ing rows of phenomena, independent of each other, so that the correspondence of representation and represented thing as well as the correspondence of the will's choice and the bodily movement is possible without ever having to assume that the mental really acts on the physical or vice versa. That, according to this view, creation is illusory theater does not seem to bother them. For Spinoza extension and thinking are the two attributes of absolute being of which we know. He does not, however, show how they can coincide in a unity either.

Thus, close at hand lies the solution for abandoning the dualistic approach by denying the full reality of one of the two modes of being in favor of the other. In this manner the monistic positions of spiritualism and mechanistic materialism arise. In spiritualism material existence is reduced to its being represented; thus, Berkeley's claim "esse est percipi" builds on the consideration that independence of existence from perception only has meaning with respect to perception and to exaggerating to an identity the relationship of appearance to existence. In this case once again God must guarantee the intersubjectivity of perception because it does not have any support in an independent existence.

137. Mechanical materialism is probably more sympathetic to people today. Descartes placed the mind responsible for science next to its object, the world of machines. Interpreting the human body as a machine naturally constituted a large research program that was slowly filled with content. In 1748 the doctor La Mettrie published a book that was conceived according to this program: *L'homme machine (The Human Being—A Machine)*. What was for Descartes a hypothetical model became a claim. Moreover, this claim seemed to be confirmed more and more through the progress of natural scientific medicine. The machine model has become a comprehensive and fruitful aid in interpreting all kinds of processes, especially due to its cybernetic extension. As long as one remains aware of its model character and, thus, its always partial and hypothetical value and re-

frains from making ontological claims, there is nothing to
which an opponent could object.

138. There are, however, several weighty arguments
against an ontological upgrading of the machine model.
1. Every mechanistic (or more generally: physicalistic) theory of mind must use expressions such as "truth," "claim,"
"sufficient explanation," and so on, in which the life of the
mind is expressed spontaneously. However, this use commits
a category mistake. 2. Physicalistic processes are introduced
as "explanations" of perception, feeling, desiring, and so on.
Such connections hold without a doubt. However, they do
not support the materialistic thesis. For such explanations
do not extend beyond the ascertainment of a factual correlation between certain chemical, and other such processes
and certain bodily capacities, modes of action, and such
without being able to derive these from the former with any
insight. The path from a theory stating true existence back
to the level of immediate experience does not succeed, but
that is exactly what is necessary for a proof of the materialistic theory. 3. There is in principle always the possibility
of technical change due to a successful physical explanation.
Even if one assumes the absurd possibility of being able to
state a physicalistic theory of "truth" or "theory," such a theory would have no practical consequences. The physicalistic physicist, in her normal research, must assume ideas such
as "knowledge" or "logical conclusion" just as "naively" as
any other "unenlightened" researcher.

The further development and partial revision of the Cartesian approach has not been able to resolve the original
perplexity. Therefore, we must problematize this approach
more thoroughly to find a solution.

3. THE REINTEGRATION OF THE BODY/PHYSICAL OBJECT INTO THE BODY AS SUCH

139. Descartes rejected as too dualistic the comparisons
through which the Platonic tradition elucidated the phenome-

nal relation of the mind to its body. "By means of these feelings of pain, hunger, thirst, and so on, nature also teaches that I am present to my body not merely in the way a seaman is present to his ship, but that I am tightly joined and, so to speak, mingled together with it, so much so that I make up one single thing with it. For otherwise, when the body is wounded, I, who am nothing but a thing that thinks, would not sense the pain. Rather, I would perceive the wound by means of the pure intellect, just as a seaman perceives by means of sight whether anything in the ship is broken" (*Meditations* VI, 13). Still, the perspective of the physicist (which the doctor has as well) has priority over the perspective of the subject that is hungry: hunger is only a kind of short form or signal for the praxis that allows us to take the correct measures (in this case, to eat something) without our being physiologists, but it is only the latter who know the true cause of the feeling of hunger and why it is helped by taking in nourishment. In this manner direct bodily feeling is interpreted technomorphically, and the radicality of the bodiliness is made harmless.

a) The Mechanism as Technomorphic Spiritualism

140. The motivation for this self-interpretation most certainly lies in the possibilities of liberating the overwhelming and dark natural powers in us, as it already had around us—to an increase in our power over our natural surroundings and ourselves. The starting point for this increase in power via technology and its corresponding sciences is a state of human beings threatened by nature that brings forth and nourishes as well as challenges and destroys human beings. That this is, in spite of it all, a constant starting point is hidden if one declares the final states of emancipation and self-positing—namely, self-knowledge and desire, on the one hand, and rationalized nature, according to the mechanic model, on the other hand—as the essence and, thus, the inner "beginning" of what "we" ourselves and nature are respectively. On the path of securing emancipated confidence

the materialistic mechanism goes one step further than the dualistic one does. For the transparency of the mind refers to the rules of its prescribed procedure. As far as its own *being* is concerned, that it exists is indubitably certain, but its origin and destination can only be accepted in trusting in the ground (God) that only hints at its (His) own existence and can be recovered neither theoretically nor practically. If, however, the principle of identity in the structure of the attainable and true does not even find its limits in the nontransparency of the spirit because this does not have any separate essence, then, in principle, *everything* can be comprehended and functionally ordered. Whoever has insight and gets involved—"we"—stands as such above and beyond the real, precisely when something standing outside the mechanical is verbally denied. The universal objectification and instrumentalization requires that the agent and beneficiary of this process does not have an essence that withdraws from the process, so that it can be completely free of all "natural vigor." Thus, the deep spiritualistic feature of technomorphic materialism becomes evident.

b) The Bodiliness of the Subject as the Foundation of Positing the Body as Thing and as Machine

141. In the following it is to be shown that, and how, the givenness "thing" and the givenness "machine" is only possible under the assumption of a more primitive bodiliness of the subject that perceives, uses, and so forth them.

A *thing* is a being of at least relative uniformity and endurance, that has a relatively stable spatial form and is perceivable and comprehensible. As such it is only conceivable for a being that lives spatially and temporally, that can see, touch, and abstractly pick up forms. The temporality of the subject has already been considered in the chapter on "Historicity." Something will be said shortly about space (see below). A few allusions, however! A thing is relative—in its appearance—to the hand-eye field. For this reason it is, insofar as it is a thing, not constituted through smells and sounds that are emitted from it or its temperature — but rather through its capacity of being grasped and seen. However, something can only be seen if it stands in the relationship of figure-background to others; and as a physical object it must stand in a perspective through which it can be related to other objects and, thus, distinguished from them. This perspective has its (functionally invisible) center in my face from which my visual field stretches. Although it lies in a sense outside of the field, there could not be any space for real things if — in another perspective — my face could not appear along with other things in the visual field of another. Still, the eye that is seen is not the functioning eye, and that remains true even when one considers that one can perceive more than simply the eyeball but also that someone is seeing. The thing appearing in the visual field awakens the expectation that it can be touched. For this a space, as was already the case with the eyes, must be measured with the body, and especially the hands: in order to overcome a distance to touch the thing, to grasp it, and so on. In order for this to be possible, I must be bodily in a similar way, that is, my body must be the immediate medium of myself, as was just said for seeing.

142. A *machine* is a thing that is constructed such that it transfers and channels forces directedly. These forces can be available through independent power generators (a waterwheel, a team of oxen, a combustion engine, an atomic power plant, etc.). In this case they complement and replace the force that is given to us primarily: our muscles. This connection retains its principled significance even when power and transmission systems are produced in contrast with which the quantity of muscle power and extent of its organic transmission system is infinitesimal — in the extreme case, only as much as is necessary for the pressing of a button. Even when a machine is able to steer itself via a built-in program and is thus not reliant upon human "service," it still belongs to the sphere of "additional apparatus" of the

body whose development began with the simplest of tools: the sphere of instruments (Lat.: *instrumentum* = tool). That the world of machines is an extension and precision of our bodiliness becomes evident through the experience of repercussion: we become (almost) as dependent on them as we are on the organs and functions of our body, that is, from the beginning oriented toward supplementation by tools and increasingly adapted to this supplementation (see Tinland 1977, 126–188). Thus, the body *can* be interpreted, from the side of its supplements, as a tool of the mind or even as a machine that has its own rules — a way of thinking that stems from the talk of "organon" (Greek: *órganon* = tool). Among these organs the hand is the most important; Aristotle calls it the "organ of organs" (*De anima* III,8 432 a1; *On the Parts of Animals* IV 687 a20), meaning, on the one hand, most important and, on the other hand, the tool due to which other tools are even possible: "tool" in the eminent sense and for this reason, taken narrowly, not merely a tool. If it were simply a tool, one would have to say which organ manipulates it. Thus, one must supplement the thought that tools are extensions of the body with the sentence that the most intimate use of tools never approaches the matter-of-course level that we have with our body in our action situations. Before I use my body or parts thereof as an instrument for the realization of special goals, it has long since functioned as a self-aimed and automatic mediation of my primary relation to the world and myself. For this reason this mediation will never be reached with the concepts of mechanical functionality, despite their suggestiveness and indispensability — not even in a different mode of conception.

4. BODILY EXISTENCE

143. A phenomenological exhibition of bodily existence is to follow the demonstration that the objectivistic and technomorphic interpretations of body did not sufficiently ac-

count for the phenomena. The subjectivity of the body must have immediately contributed to the approach: "body" is—in contrast to the objectively present physical object—always the body of a subject. It is always the object of an actual, never merely potential, possession. This possession is always individual, never collective (so that the body is always my body or your body, and so on, but never our body). Our topic can, therefore, be, not the body as such, but rather the possession of the body or the bodily existence of the human subject.

The philosophical thematization of bodily existence occurs on two levels that, ultimately, cannot strictly be kept apart: on the level of the description of the modes of how the body is experienced and on the level of the ontological interpretation of the experienced matter. The failure of the Cartesian ontology of body as an extended thing pushes us back to the level of experience and then demands the working out of new ontological categories. Before we make several observations on the ontology of the body, two selected dimensions of bodiliness are to be briefly described: spatial and sexual bodily existence.

a) Spatial Existence in the Body

144. Every space refers to something that is or can be *in* it. It is space for. . . . Even empty space is influenced by what was removed from it (and for what it was removed). From this it follows that there are numerous spaces. There is no "one" space, in unity and absoluteness.

In the case what space makes room for is a subject, then certain determinations of space arise that abstract stereo-metric-physical space cannot have: orientation, actual volume, distances. The scientifically conceived space of geometry and even relativistic physics does not have an up or down, no front or back, no left or right: it knows no expanse or narrowness, no closeness or distance, no privileged status of particular places over others—no places at all! It lies beyond the difference between inside and outside. In other words, space as it is scientifically conceived does not have what characterizes it as the space of a subject. For our way of existing spatially all of the mentioned differences are fundamental. The surveyor can place the origin point of her coordinate system anywhere and direct the axes in any direction; for no point of her three-dimensional place-manifold and no direction of a line that could run through any of these points are somehow privileged. (Taken strictly, talking of "anywhere" or "direction" is already anthropomorphic.) For our way of life every possible point of reference refers to the origin where we stand measuring—and every possible coordinate system is rooted in the system of dimensions that stretch up and down, front and back, left and right from me. The separation of the directions in areas of nontransferable, even contrasting, meaning is fundamental for the spatiality of space. For it is through this that the voluminous free space opens up and extends, which I am measuring, in movement, long before I begin to measure out paths, surfaces, and volumes. The organization of space and the orientation of my bodily existence constitute the two sides of one phenomenon (see Straus 1964).

145. When we begin to think about space, we are so settled on the clearly arranged visual space that one must first become aware through practice of what it means to traverse, experience, and fulfill a space. There are spaces that confine us, bordering on uneasiness, and there are spaces in which we feel isolated, bordering on agoraphobia. In the middle lie the snug protecting "caves" and the widening halls. According to how we feel, our surroundings can appear larger or smaller to us, we can fill spaces confidently or we can live in a snail's house in which we move through different spaces. Walls at our backs that we suddenly imagine falling back force us to take a step forward. On the spot of the (imaginary) support arises on (imaginary) gaping hole. We experience round rooms (or spaces) differently than rectangular ones, long rooms differently than square ones. Land-

scapes can mean much to one: areas with the kind of landscape in which we grew up perhaps foremost.

146. The various spaces in which we live are not at all
only different parcels of one single space. If we abstract from
the modifications of our subjective experience of space, various realms of life are distinguished objectively through physical and symbolic borders: my house or room of spaces that
belong to you, a third party, or no one; the public street and
the store with its border; church and station halls; villa and
slum neighborhoods; first and last place; one's home or foreign country; cultural meccas and desert. What is acceptable,
normal, or forbidden at one place is eccentric or looked down
upon at another. Symmetrically situated buildings, gardens,
and cities give rise to a different atmosphere than those asym-
metrically situated with several centers. All of these differences in meaning work with the immanent differences in
meaning that are peculiar to a human being's living spaces.

147. Thus, the rich use of spatial metaphors in our
language is not something that was added later and from
the "outside" to the original, merely literal use; rather the
"high" is not only higher from the start but also better than
the "low." We can feel lost or constricted not merely in physical spaces but also in social spaces (see No. 129). Mere bodily presence is compatible with the absence of consciousness; the traveler who has arrived at his trip's destination
often needs some time in order to let "his soul catch up."
Arriving at full bodily presence is more than the mere presence of the body or cognitive ascertainment of the place at
which one finds oneself.

148. We are bodily spatial, in a space. However, we are
also "in" our body which we invigorate from its center out-
ward into the extremities—whereby this center, according
to the character and situation, can lie in the area of the
diaphragm, in the upper chest, or between the eyes. One can
crawl into and tense up one's body, let one's upper body slump
over or pull oneself together. Sometimes one has to search
for some human beings, hidden deep in their body. Others

are completely there in bodily expression. Children are in their bodies differently than adolescents in puberty, and these differently than adults, males different than females, with various phenomena of intermediary stages. The elderly and sick leave their body "inwardly," so that it increasingly becomes a mere "shell."

We do not have to orient ourselves in our bodies the way we do in places (although it is true to a certain extent here as well). There is a system of automatic spatial orientation and movement coordination that functions properly through learning and practice but is already latently given (see Schilder 1923). Existence-in-the-body and existence-in-space belong together, whereby existence in the elbow-room of the body has a relative priority. Our body is the place that we must already have taken up in order to be able to take up places. I can exist in spaces only because I am ultimately *in* my body such that I *am* myself my body.

b) Sexual Bodily Existence

149. Giving a comprehensive theory of sexuality is not the present intent. Sexual action is only to be taken as an example of an action in which the body—as an impulse—is the subject and not merely a tool of agency. We are referring to sexual impulse because, on the one hand, the search for nourishment has become superfluous and is thus not experienced as impulsive any more, and, on the other hand, sexual impulse as the "most spiritual of all impulses" (Nietzsche) stands closer to the acting ego and its dynamics than all of the other impulses.

Not only the hand but also the reproductive organs have a right to the title of being the tool of tools, a tool par excellence—if one looks at what is brought forth through their action. If, however, one looks at the kind of relationship that exists between the agent and her hand, and the agent and her sexual organs, then it is the case that the hand must sooner be called a tool (*órganon*) than the sexual organ.

For in actions with the hands the subject stands with greater sovereignty over his actions than is the case for reproduction (and whatever belongs in this realm). The will, directed by insight into functionality, can carry out each single phase of action itself and, for this reason, can separate them or break them off. In the sexual act this is not the case, for one finds oneself on a single arc of movement that can be distracted or broken off, but whose dynamic cannot be (re)-started at any phase simply through an act of will. In contrast to technical production one finds oneself fascinated or excited (a state belonging in the realm of natural reproduction), even before one consciously and intentionally becomes involved in something. Of course, most of the time there is the possibility of the failure of continuing the already begun action or of finishing it in this or that way, but the impulse remains primary. It cannot simply be replaced by a free-floating want. It gives us the power for a capability that we cannot otherwise produce for ourselves — for a capability to which we only have access to a certain degree because, without the interference of free choice, it actualizes itself.

150. The high-handedness of sexual dynamics can be experienced to such a degree that the thought can come to mind whether we, the agents, are not the mere tool of a super-human natural impulse (see Schopenhauer's chapter entitled "Metaphysics of Sexual Love" from *The World as Will and Idea* II, chapter 44). This thought is the exact reflection of the idea of the independence of the freely acting subject that has access to the beginning of all of its dynamics — and is a limiting construct just as the former is. Of course, sexual love has a power and goal that is autonomous and not given through our choice and cannot simply be subjected to other goals. However, this is an argument only against the absolute autonomy of the agent that posits itself, not against its relative autonomy. For this reason, seen from the perspective of the ego, there remains an ambivalence in sexual impulse: we experience ourselves as carried to a fascinating reality that is experienced as something good and as fulfilling

the lust for life and love—and at the same time carried in a direction in which we do not want to go. The power that acts even when we do not want it to is the same power that gives our desires range and strength. The old, Platonic metaphor of the horse and rider that was picked up by Freud and Scheler, Kandinski and Marino Marini, reflects the state of affairs better than the metaphor of tool and technician.

Other modes of moving oneself such as walking, dancing, jumping, and so on are to be interpreted in an analogous manner to the realm of sexual modes of action. Everywhere the concern is the further formation of an already structured, natural-autonomous dynamics. We must let it rest with these few allusions.

c) Ontological Scientific-theoretical Questions

151. The science that is concerned with the human body more than any other is medicine. Its spectacular progress in the last decades relies upon whatever limitation in the human body is comprehensible for the natural sciences: the mechanical, electrical, chemical, physiological, and other states and processes that can be comprehended with respect to their functionality (or disfunctionality) as proper functioning, that is, health. It seems significant that health itself is seen as the relative absence of sickness, since it, despite being positive, can only be conceived from its being threatened and lacking and, for the practice of healing, is best envisaged in such a manner. Sickness and health are states of the organism that, on the one hand, are experienced directly but, on the other hand, can also be determined through certain objective indications (temperature, blood pressure, etc.). The question "How do you feel?" and the study of the blood and so on belong together. For what the prolapse speed means can only be explained through its connection with physiological theory. However, what a physiological theory explains are correlations between objective factors, and these correlations explain a change in the subjective state. The

objectification of a body to a relatively closed functional whole ("machine") has as its occasion the search for the natural causes of the loss of health or death. It has its enduring embedment in the modes of immediate bodily existence and experience. The object of medical theory is thus a well-founded construction, not a pure thing in itself.

152. The same is naturally true, although to an even greater extent, of all of the subdivisions of medical theory—of the observation of the body as a mechanical system, in the sense of the Cartesian *res extensa*. Of course, there are systems of physical objects (in the astronomical and mechanical realms) that—as it seems—can be exhaustively described with the means of mechanics. With respect to the human body it is true that mechanical description and explanation, which is meaningful and possible, are only concerned with an abstract dimension. The mechanical structure is the frame and foundation for a construct that, as such, is lived and interpreted by other laws. That they arise here as well as there does not imply that it constitutes the true essence of the one or the other, for the truth is concrete—and in the concretion of the human body the physical truth is only a partial and abstract one.

153. The body can be researched in the natural sciences —but a theory of body as such cannot be one of natural science. It falls, seen in a Cartesian framework, in between and in the mixed area of the *res extensa* and *res cogitans*. The thematization of the body problem from the side of doctors (not seldom from a psychiatrist such as Viktor v. Weizsäcker and his school), who saw a narrowing in the exclusive natural science character of medicine, oftentimes runs a battle against the intellectual dualism of our culture that Descartes initiated philosophically. The same is naturally true of the philosophical attempts at primitively describing the mixed areas in between the *res extensa* and *res cogitans*. It is no accident that Husserl's phenomenology, proceeding from Cartesian premises, reaches a border precisely in the theory of the consciousness of body that his students could

only overcome by revising the whole foundation of the ego-logical philosophy of consciousness. Thus, they did not only doubt that the true existence of the perceivable world could be reduced to mathematical constructs but also that all consciousness (in the widest sense) could be reduced to a pure, self-constructing ego (see Zaner 1964). The thematization of the problem of bodily essence, thus, leads into the center of ontology. Despite all anti-Cartesianism — rather, precisely for this reason — one remains bound to the basic Cartesian attitude and does not return to an ancient Greek conception according to which the body and soul were the real constituents of the whole human being. One sticks with the distinctions between different modes of consciousness or givenness or language.

The theoretical "possession" of what functions as a body points back to the living possession of my body, and this, further, to a fundamental bodily existence (see Marcel). The otherness that implies the experiencing and practical possession of the body is not the most fundamental. However, the fundamental aspect, the identity, is not closed in itself but is rather a ground for a possible relation of possession. In the back and forth between having a body and being a body lies human bodiliness. Neither Nietzsche's phrase "I am completely body" nor Sartre's interpretation of the body as the contingent form of my contingence finds the center of its mark.

C. The Mental Element of the Act of Existence

154. In Part B the issue at hand was the basic dimensions of the act of human existence, and, because the other than ourselves belongs to this act, the issue was also the basic dimensions of the world in which we each live as well as everything that we encounter and belongs to us. In the part that follows, the "how," or the manner, of this act is the topic insofar as it deals with specifically human acts. Higher animals fulfill the criteria that we established for the application of the existential-predicate "subject" (see No. 27–30). The peculiar aspect of human subjectivity lies in the "how" of the act: human existence is not merely a relation but rather lives this relation such that the formation of a second relation belongs to this relation (see Kierkegaard, *Sickness unto Death,* IAa). A human being does not merely stand in a perceptual relation to some things; rather she knows that she is perceiving. A human being does not merely have a manifold of capacities to act in practical situations but is also related through a capacity of a second order to these capacities. He does both of these, if he does them at all—since there are prehuman elements in human behavior as well,

due to his position within the realm of the mental. Just as water is essential for the life of a fish, the mental is essential (albeit not the only essential element) for human life. The mental aspect of human beings is a constitutive capacity for that self-relation whose basic modes carry the name "consciousness" and "freedom" and whose consideration constitutes both of the chapters of this part C. This already gives a hint as to what the element of the mental is in itself.

I. Mental Consciousness

Our considerations are arranged in three sections here. First (1), we shall be concerned to note the phenomenon of consciousness, to articulate several of its basic structures, and to defend it from tempting reductions. Sense perceptual knowledge shall serve as our example. In the second section (2), the narrowness that almost invariably arose due to our orientation to this example must be widened in various directions. Finally (3), we ask, with transcendental intent, about the nature of consciousness—thus, of the human being.

1. THE "PHENOMENON" OF CONSCIOUS-NESS

155. The first step in the interpretation of something must always consist in getting a good look at it, that is, finding access to the experience in which this thing is given (more or less) primitively. "Given" is, however, related to "consciousness." Something being given means approximately that one is conscious or aware of something. How is one conscious of consciousness? Certainly not in the same way that certain states of affairs become conscious for someone. Consciousness itself is apparently a thing of a different order than certain states of affairs of which we can be aware or conscious. We cannot thematize it directly but rather must take a detour with three intermediary steps: (a) the fictitious visualization of unconsciousness, (b) the analysis of a spe-

cial example, (c) and the defense from simplified attempts at interpretation.

a) The "Wonder" of Conscious-ness

156. Someone loses consciousness due to a collapse of the circulatory system, anesthesia, falling asleep, or otherwise. He is un-conscious: he lies there peacefully as if sleeping or dead or he cannot be approached. At any rate he does not notice anything that is happening around and in himself. One recognizes this through his behavior. How is it, however, for him, in his unconscious condition, to be unconscious? The question is absurd by definition insofar as one is asking about the consciousness of unconsciousness. Perhaps there is some such experience of unconsciousness in certain meditative states insofar as an experience of a pure self-consciousness, free of all content, is present. The absence of content in consciousness would be the common element between true unconsciousness and meditative emptiness. Still, a continuous consciousness remains during the "sinking" experiences as the basis of varying modes of consciousness whose difference becomes clear in this change without illuminating the nature of consciousness via the experience of its opposite. This last remark is naturally true for the transition from the state of unconsciousness to that of consciousness (and vice versa) as well. Neither falling asleep nor waking up can be experienced with awareness. Consciousness is something primary which cannot be transgressed. It defines essentially the human mode of life. It has a similar power and inconspicuousness for our existence as air is for our breathing, only much more radical because very deeply rooted. Although we can delineate consciousness as it is in others (or in ourselves in retrospect) by describing its difference from unconsciousness by noting the difference in behavior patterns, we are not in a position to draw such a distinction in the field of our immediate experience, so that consciousness may appear to be nothing at all—that is how incomprehensible it is.

157. Still, that there is something like consciousness at all is something quite surprising. Normally we are so taken in by the contents we are conscious of that we do not notice anything of the consciousness itself. That belongs to the dynamic structure of human consciousness, and it is perfectly well this way. It is only on reflection that we notice that the different contents that are factually very different are interconnected as conscious thoughts into a unity of my stream of consciousness. Since I myself, as an "empirical ego" (with respect to my bodily and mental states and processes), belong to such contents, and since I can make myself understood to others (and vice versa), the unity of consciousness is not the unity of the individual in the sense that I, this individual, have an inner unity. Through the contrast between, on the one hand, the variety of the conscious contents and the unity of consciousness and, on the other hand, the plurality of the conscious subjects and the unity of the common conscious thoughts, consciousness itself becomes the topic on a first level of thematization. It becomes a "phenomenon," the object of a new kind of attention. Due to the thematization of something of which all thematizations are just specific modes, we are amazed—an amazement that does not recede upon further consideration but rather increases. For upon further reflection one of the things we take for granted and with which the cement of our spontaneous theoretical beliefs is armed dissolves.

158. One of those beliefs we take for granted and comes to mind immediately if we ask ourselves what reality consists in is: reality is the totality of all things, whereby the things, organized material complexes, interact with one another. That this (or a similar) answer would spontaneously come to mind and persist with psychological stubbornness if we have recognized its merely relative character—this is not mere chance but rather grounded in the organization of our psyche. Within the cosmos of our sense apparatus the auditory, tactile, and, especially, visual senses dominate. What (distinguished from others in its form) can be seen, touched, and has a central position in the manifold of the sensually

perceivable. Sensuality and motor skills are integrated for all living organisms into a single functioning unit such that the sensual givenness receives its significance (and, thus, its possible extent and clear boundaries) from the necessity of proper reactions to what is useful or harmful for the particular organism. The human being can sometimes extract her senses from their operational function for motor skills and, for example, just look and let it be at that (Greek: *theorein*). For the visual sense this occurs more naturally and frequently than for the other senses, and if something can be both seen and touched, it counts as reality for us. As soon as the senses are theoretical, the equation arises: reality = perceptually real presence.

159. What is this real presence itself? The question has two meanings. On the one hand, it refers to the nature of the things as they are in themselves. Thus, it is a basic question in ontology. On the other hand, it refers to consciousness, that is, conscious being or existence of the things for you or me—to its being-for an eye and -for a hand that are the first realizations and pictures for the mental view and grasp. What consciousness ultimately is is again an ontological question. In our anthropological approach we are referred to an ontological clarification of the question. Once again, we have an occasion in which the "reactive" character (gathering and evaluating results) of anthropology in relation to other, more basic philosophical disciplines is revealed. Yet, we can and must prepare for this ontological clarification, and it cannot be achieved without an analysis of human consciousness. Beforehand, however, a trick, an attempt at fiction, can help lure the fact of consciousness into consciousness.

160. I can imagine that I have always been blind, deaf, had no tactile or olfactory sensations, and so on but am otherwise quite normal, equipped with the capacity to reflect. What would the real world, the world as it is in itself, be *for me?* In what would *my world* consist? After I have become accustomed to such a state, I can then imagine how

it would be if slowly, one by one, the doors to my senses were opened. What I would experience, the event of becoming aware, can serve as a metaphorical indication of the non-derivative amazement of consciousness itself that was assumed in our fantasy game as a formal consciousness. (One can also imagine living in a soundproof room, which is at first dampened and then suddenly normalized, or a dark night that is permeated by daylight. Thus, we have the old picture of light as the third element that carries vision and the visual into its reality, for example, Plato, *Republic* VI, 18–19.) Terminologically we should note that we use the expression "consciousness" in a wide sense, so that it is equivalent with awareness. If the context admits of it, that is, if we want to emphasize consciousness as a mode of being or existence, be it of the object or the subject, we will write the word with a hyphen, conscious-ness.

b) Structures of Perceptual Consciousness

161. As an example of a particular consciousness we will analyze the consciousness accompanying a case of visual perception. It can be expressed, again as an example, in the following sentence: "The chestnut tree has already started to bud" and then in the sentence "I see (i.e., have seen) that the chestnut tree has already started to bud." (For the meantime we can abstract from the question as to what extent consciousness is possible prior to its linguistic formulation; see No. 53–57 and No. 180–184. For this analysis we must at any rate assume a linguistically influenced, even if not necessarily spoken, form of consciousness.)

162. The primary form of consciousness—in our example —is objective: the becoming aware, that is, the appearing, of an objective state of affairs. In this mode of consciousness I am completely engrossed by the object through which my consciousness flourishes by becoming aware of it. If I am not engrossed by the object, do not lose myself in concentrating on the object (in order to become aware of one

of its determinations), then there is no perception. I, as the perceiver, do not appear in the form of consciousness, although nothing is perceived (as such) without (a not necessarily expressed) perceptual intent. Thus, I am somehow included in objective consciousness. The continuous transition from the one (merely objective) form of consciousness to the other (reflexive, I-related) witnesses to that. Since it was *I* who flourished in the perceived object, forgetting myself, and since this flourishing is not a submersion, but rather an act of subjectivity, consciousness slides quite easily from its objective form, that is only accomplished by a trace of preawareness of self-consciousness, into the form of reflexive consciousness of myself, as one perceives this or that. I can remember that I saw the ship at that time, although I was not expressly aware of it at the time that *I* saw it, but rather only that it *was there.* The content of consciousness, in the one case, is the ship (in its existence); in the other, the vision (of the ship in its existence). The transition from the one mode to the other occurs through the bending around and mirroring back (re-flection) of the consciousness, sunken in its object, to its own act-ual reality centered in myself. That is only possible because a primitive being-at-oneself belongs to consciousness. Of course, the naive unity with the perceived object is always prior (temporally) to the reflection of the perceiving and the having-perceived, but in itself, in the order of being, perception relies on a primitive, essential being-at-oneself of the perceiver, due to which he can either live in the object or move back from it to himself in reflection.

163. This primitive being-at-oneself that constitutes the roots of consciousness is not itself a conscious content, much less the conscious-ness of certain physical or mental properties that I have. For express self-consciousness, filled with content, is already a very specific form of consciousness which in its entirety is made possible by this primitive, ontological being-at-oneself—and this can itself be, not the object of an immediate consciousness insofar as it enables all concrete consciousness, but rather only, in later remembering (in Plato's

sense), the object of abstract speculative knowledge that moves from the justified to the justification.

c) Refutation of False Interpretations

164. A unity of perceived and perception, of object and subject, lies in perception. The ambiguity of the word "perception," which can mean either the thing that is perceived or the act of perceiving, points toward a surprising identity that is present here: namely, that the perceived object and the perceiver are identical (see Aristotle, *De anima* III,7 431 a1). Object and subject are correlative relation concepts; expressed grammatically, a genitive (or possessive) always belongs to them: object *of* a perception, an attempt, and so on, and subject *of* a perception that is directed toward an object. If one overlooks this point, one might attempt to understand being perceived from the side of the perceiving subject or, conversely, the perception from the side of the perceived object, whereby subject and object are taken as something objective or quasi-objective and deprived of their special mode of relationality. Both interpretations, while complementing each other, are incorrect attempts to get by the issue, assuming this mysterious identity as an irreducible fact. Let's critically evaluate the objectivistic interpretation first and then move on to consider the subjectivistic one! (See also No. 136–138.)

165. Objectivism recognizes only those kinds of things and relations that are presented in the objectively perceivable world. It attempts to interpret the fact of perceptual consciousness by the categorical means of objective knowledge of material states of affairs. Thus, it conceives of perception as a relation between two things, whereby the perceived thing acts on the perceiving thing, so that a picture, a subjective representation of the first thing, arises in the second. This interpretation, taken from philosophical common sense, can be further differentiated with the help of scientific knowledge. That, then, translates into a picture whereby

certain lightwaves proceed (or are reflected) from the chestnut tree, and, if I look in this direction, are bound together by the lens of my eye and projected onto the retina. With the eye's sensitive rods and cones the differential light energy is transferred into electrical voltage differences, whose interaction, transmitted cybernetically through the functioning of the central nervous system many times, finally brings forth my representation of the chestnut tree.

166. The partial explanations that are given in this connection with the methods of physics (wave theory, optics, electricity, etc.), chemistry, physiology, and such are to be neither discussed at present nor doubted. They state the conditions under which human perception stands. If they change or do not hold at all, perception becomes impossible or changes its way (going blind through cataracts; color changes through different lighting or quick movement or backgrounds with different colors; etc.). However, what about the claim of explaining perceptual knowledge as such? This claim must be disputed. For the path from the conditioned, that is, the perception, to its diverse (not at all exhaustively listed) conditions is taken, but the decisive path back, through which it becomes comprehensible how perception results from all of these conditions, is disrupted. The relation between physical sight and psychological sight is only possible because both are related to the same object, namely, the perception as it is given in naive reflection. The test person must always be asked, "What do you see now?" (when the experimenter has changed the conditions). There is, however, a lacuna between the end station of physical-physiological reconstruction (the flickering of stimulation patterns in the visual center of the brain) and the "picture" that is to be produced in one's head (see Eccles 1984). If we did not know, through the correlation of brain injuries, artificial stimulations, and so on with certain visual defects, blackouts of vision, and hallucinations, that there is a connection between the functioning of the brain and the ability to perceive, the brain would remain a com-

plete mystery for us, just as the bones in the ear and the localization of the sense of taste in the tongue were for earlier generations. Therefore, the objectivistic theory of perception does not really explain what perception is, but rather what an eye, ear, brain, and so on is, how it is built, and why it must be built in that way in order to fulfill the function which it serves under normal conditions.

167. The same is true for the evolutionary interpretation of perceptual knowledge that has been presented, for example, by K. Lorenz (1977), G. Vollmer (1975 and 1985), and R. Riedl (1984): that we can normally trust our senses is justified, according to this conception, because the (physiological and psychological) organization of our senses has developed as a part of those dispositions and fixtures that have enabled our survival through mutation and natural selection over numerous millions of years. The truth of our perceptual knowledge (or even knowledge in general) would then lie in the fact that reality can be grasped insofar as it is necessary for our survival. The a priori forms of our spatial representations or objective perception are not to be equated with the structures of being. This is all quite clear, especially when one looks, not at knowledge in general, but rather at the primary form of sense perception for its genesis in an evolutionary theoretical explanation—a limitation that the authors do not always uphold, which, however, must be respected if one wants to avoid accepting that evolutionary epistemology only possesses the amount of truth that is necessary for survival. Still, for sensuality itself one must keep these limits in perspective: Is it not surprising that the emergence of an organization of senses that is only oriented toward survival has brought forth a sensuality whose highest achievements lie in the realm of the useless (art, music, culinary art, and so on) and is, thus, more related to theoretical, impractical knowledge? Especially, however—and this is what is important for our purposes—this theory, even in its best form, can make as little sense of the fact of percep-

tual knowledge as the physical and other theories pertain-
ing to the present functioning of the sense apparatus (see
Frey 1980, Baumgartner 1981).

168. Subjectivism is the flip side of objectivism. If, namely,
the objectivist idea of an adequate cause of a representation
through chemical stimulation and such is taken seriously,
then there is no reason why what arises should be understood
as a "picture," an inner-mental representation of a somehow
similar reality, as the naive person off the street believes—
although only for the visual sense. Perception is not the reception of truth anymore. Its true object is not the real but
rather a representation that appears to be representing something real, yet it is in fact only the reflection of a change in
one's bodily state in the screen "consciousness" beyond whose
"immanence," that is, to the "things in themselves," we can
never come.

169. Two other subjectivistic arguments run in this same
skeptical direction, although not as far. Because sense deception can occur, it can be claimed that, in principle, there
is a gap between the sense representation and the represented
thing so that we would, at first, only be dealing with representations without ever being certain whether objective states
of affairs are represented in them. Against this one can reply
that we can resolve sense deceptions and that we could not
know and thus not doubt anything about them if we did not
normally have access to reality. The second argument relies
on the dependence of our manner of perception on the contingent organization of our sense organs. A fly's eyes present visual objects differently than a human's eyes. One should
add that we can reflect upon this conditioned state, in principle at least, and thus can guard against a premature identification between the mode of appearance of reality in the
medium of our senses and the mode of reality in itself. Again,
in the capacity to reflect upon the fact of being conditioned
lies a relation to reality. (In order to determine what this could
be in more detail, one would have to address the question
whether it is so certain that human sensuality is one pos-

sible organization of senses in addition to others and *just as* contingent for the admitted reality as it is for other animals in similar surrounding conditions.) Nevertheless, both of these arguments rest on difficulties that can be removed; one need not become a skeptic due to them.

170. Whoever maintains a causal theory of perception must arrive at skeptical conclusions — if one does not notice the contradiction within one's own theory first. The contradiction lies in the fact that, on the one hand, knowledge of physical processes, as they proceed in themselves, is claimed; on the other hand, the truth value of all representations is rescinded. One cannot save oneself from the contradiction by demoting the physical theory to mere subjective validity. For in that case it is either idle talk from which nothing follows and which one does not believe in practice — or the beginning of the insight that the methods of a physical or other such theory cannot explain the essence or nature, rather only partial moments of the known reality that lie within the realm of ascertainability for the senses. If, however, there exists real, intersubjective, pertinent perceptual knowledge, which nobody *seriously* doubts, then it arises, regardless of all possible mediation through representations, subjective horizons, and so on, by the aimed-for knowledge being identical with the state of affairs that reveals itself (to our senses). This identity assumes ontologically that I, as an actual epistemological subject, become identical with the state of affairs. It is only from this identity that preliminary, superficial, distorted, and false conceptions can be seen as such. It is only in this manner that we can relativize the way that we (contemporary, English-speaking human beings) can behave epistemologically toward the states of affairs. The manner of the "bodily" present of the state of affairs will of course always be determined by our mode of perception, so that we can never grasp the states of affairs (things) as they would reveal themselves in a purely mode-less, infinite epistemic space in themselves. Nonetheless, finite knowledge remains knowledge of the state of affairs itself, and thus a true

identification in which the difference between inside (the "immanence of consciousness") and outside (that which "transcends consciousness") ceases to exist.

2. DIMENSIONS OF CONSCIOUSNESS

What has been said about the "phenomenon" of consciousness (that can exist as a phenomenon only on the different levels of reflection) must be clarified in various respects. Our example, consciousness of visual perception, will be relativized insofar as it is embedded in a broader context.

a) Spontaneity and Receptivity in Consciousness

171. The process of perception and the knowledge that results from it can be described as progressive permeation into the state of affairs that is revealing itself and, at the same time, as progressive dismantling of improper opinions as well as the illusionary desires that carry them. The state of affairs should be brought into the realm of appearances by becoming perceived and known. Herein lie receptivity (passivity) as well as spontaneity (activity) in all levels of perception and knowing.

172. There is passivity because all knowledge is receiving through one of its senses. The states of affairs already have a determinateness before we determine them in knowledge. The latter determination has the purpose of a "repetition" of the former. The concepts of truth and falsity, adequacy and inadequacy, depend on the priority of being over knowing. The receiving is, however, a taking, thus, something spontaneous, no purely passive impression like with playdoh. It is an exploration or opening of oneself. Already the lowest level of sensation is enabled through a relation to the self, through an active differentiation from others, and, thus, through a reference to everything that one can receive. After this prelevel of consciousness the next mode

of spontaneity can be called vague attention. Without it
nothing is perceived if it does not strongly stimulate: one
cannot see what lies in front of oneself, not hear what is
said as long as one is not mentally "there." This "there-ness"
or presence is an achievement, an act of spontaneity. Further yet, there is a directed attention in which whatever might
be revealed in the object is tentatively anticipated. In this "intention" a pretext is given to the revealing of a thing, the
pretext of a certain way of appearing.

On all levels of perception and the knowledge that arises
from it there is a kind of question-and-answer game. Without the pretext of a question nothing is revealed. Without
anything capable of being revealed any question is senseless.

173. Every question already has a determinedness about
it. It arises when the unlimited emptiness and openness for
the possibility of or desire for knowledge is contracted into
a limited form. This is true on the level of intentional and
consciously asked questions as well as natural questions of
the pressing reality that already lies within the structure of
our sensual mental activity as such. In every question there
is an hypothesis (presumption of an answer), an anticipation as to possible truth. Thus, two different kinds of such
anticipations can be distinguished: on the one hand, special, freely constructed hypotheses and, on the other hand,
universal, object constitutive pretexts. The former are to serve
as a path to the latter!

The telephone rings. "That is Mrs. Reese.— Oh, it's you,
Heather . . . !"—"Munich's city hall reminds me of Brussels',
but a lot of things are quite different, for example. . . ."
Specific expectations are formulated and then either confirmed, falsified, or forced into further differentiation by the
(first, renewed or deepened) perception in the realm of directed attention. The expectations have several levels. My
"hypothesis" regarding the person calling implies the hypothetical certainty that anyone is calling at all (instead of the
ringing being called forth by manipulation in the telephone
exchange). This implies, once again, the hypothetical cer-

tainty that it has rung at all (and that the ringing was not hallucinated by me).

174. All particular hypotheses can be shown to be correct or incorrect (if they are formulated with reference to possible experience). The universal, object constitutive pretexts, however, are not veri- and falsifiable, because they refer, not to the content, but rather to the form of a revealing. The concern is, among other things, that of being, being determined in itself—the idea of being caused by something— the idea of the difference between reality and possibility— the idea of the vaguely good—the structural factors of the space and time of perception and experience. Several of these pretexts belong to each pretext like the idea of being. Others are very general but only refer to a certain region of perceptual knowledge, like the idea of causality or the idea of something-with-properties or the idea of the whole-in-its-parts or the idea of the means to its end. (To have a classification here is the task of ontology and a theory of transcendental objects that further develop the Aristotelian and Kantian teachings of the forms of statements. The anthropological interest is in the existence of such pretexts.)

175. The content of these pretexts is not gained through experience. That we can talk about them we owe to the fact that they can be abstractly taken out of the context of perceptual knowledge. However, that they are in such a context results from "our" letting the object of perception as such (i.e., the perception of the object) come into existence with their help. "Our": that means, not us as the origin of conscious and intentional actions, rather us as the carriers of a natural tendency toward knowledge. That does not mean that these formal pretexts are already available for the small infant. Learning in this field is just the development of an innate capability whereby this development need not occur in every culture and linguistic community in the same way. "Innate" is a negative concept in this context and means approximately "not simply acquired." To what extent the "have always had" can be interpreted biologically (genetically and

through evolution) we have already discussed briefly above. What is completely certain is that the idea of being-in-itself, that is, the dynamo and enabling of all self-critical doubting of truth and the ultimate validity of our initially believed opinions, lies beyond all biological explanation—and that is naturally true for its correlate, consciousness as such.

176. The perception and the knowledge that results from it is a layered act that sketches a free space for revealing—a striving that fulfills itself by revealing itself. In this fulfillment, as particular and preliminary as it may be, spontaneity and receptivity are one. The subject flourishes in the object and vice versa. Only a person who does not know the (transcendental) "prehistory" of every object of perception and knowledge can still think that one can understand the reality of the epistemological subject (as such) from the reality that presents itself as objective—as a mere subclass of it.

b) Theoretical and Practical Consciousness

177. One of the highest forms of perception (Greek: *aisthesis*) is aesthetic perception: the Epicurean absorption of oneself in a beautiful appearance that reposes in itself. It is not surprising that one limits the concept of aesthetics to the visual and audio. Culinary pleasures do not belong to aesthetics. Where one perceives aesthetically, one looks and listens without a practical intent; rather, looking and listening are sufficient ends in themselves. This is true in a similar manner for the form of consciousness involved in theoretical knowledge. This, too, is desired for its own sake (see Aristotle, *Metaphysics* I,1). The Greek word "*theoría*" originally means "looking."

This should not tempt one into restricting consciousness to mere theoretical consciousness that finds its fulfillment in mental sense perception of something that is a true being-in-itself. In addition to theoretical consciousness there is practical consciousness. One becomes aware in practical consciousness, not what the things are in themselves, rather what they can or should be for me (and my possible actions). In this realm my duties, possibilities, and so on arise. I become aware of a chance, a threat, an offer, or a dangerous situation, not as a disinterested observer, but rather as a participant. The quality of awareness that dominates here is not that of being, but rather that of good and evil (in the whole gamut of variations of good and evil). The dominance of the good does not exclude the element of being: "It is very cold in this room!" is an objective statement, and instead of being exhausted in its objective message, it may additionally contain an implicit request to turn on the heat, because one might be afraid of catching a cold.

178. Consciousness in a practical context is basic when compared with consciousness in the merely "looking" sense. For one should not forget that the senses and motor skills form a single functional unit (see Straus 1956) that, in turn, is comprehensible from the liveliness of life: in the face of new situations and having to search for new answers in order to live and to make the best out of life. Life is essentially moving forward, while pure looking (in the theoretical sense) is significant in itself and, as a partial anticipation of resting at an end, can only be a break, a temporary interruption, for the duration of the path.

179. Practical consciousness, having one subjective and one objective pole, just as theoretical consciousness does, can occur in two ways that permeate each other in concrete cases: in a technical-practical way and in a moral-practical way. In the technical-practical (or also: pragmatic) consciousness the concern is with know-how. Contained in it are the present realities with reference to a future goal as well as the means and paths to its realization: the grasp of a situation and understanding how to act that leads to the desired goal. An extension and differentiation of this consciousness proceed through the acquisition of general, but practically applicable, knowledge of all kinds (life experience, education in a craft or in supervising people, technical sciences). In

the moral-practical consciousness, conversely, the concern is the judgment of the possible or already initiated goals of actions. Its basic form is consciousness that prohibits, commands, and invites. The moral-practical consciousness as well as the pragmatic consciousness can be expressed in sentences that show no structural difference from the theoretical statements. It does not follow from this that one may neglect the difference between theoretical-descriptive and practical sentences. The truth has a different character, and the conditions for becoming aware of the different states of affairs are different. Everyone knows of the highly educated, theoretical intellectual who is not capable of dealing with people and cars as well as the experienced practitioner whose moral sensitivity has remained an underdeveloped territory. Having studied a textbook in psychology does not mean that one knows how it applies to oneself—and vice versa. Today the nontheoretical modes of consciousness, knowledge, and education are not taken into consideration enough, and the intellectual modes are overestimated. Reflection upon the peculiarity and indispensability of the modes of practical consciousness is, thus, important for a balanced conscious culture.

c) Levels of Consciousness

180. Until now we have almost always been considering complete, that is, linguistically formulated, but not further analyzable, perceptions. A kind of middle position of consciousness is defined through such perceptions, but which still, as such, has higher and lower positions, that is, prelevels and raised levels, of consciousness around it.

181. Different modes of prelevels of consciousness can be cited. A first mode concerns the background of objective consciousness which does not stand in the light of the express attention of consciousness, not the actual topic, but is related to the topic such that it must somehow be contained in consciousness along with the topic. The basso os-

tinato in a polyphonic piece in which I only follow the melody is, for example, of such a mode—or the main branches of a tree that I glance at in order to see whether it is an oak or ash tree. If the bass were not there at all, or differently, I would hear the melody differently as well. Thus, I "picked it up" without it entering my consciouness in a way that I could make a statement about it.

182. A second mode of preconsciousness concerns knowledge or memory that is not present in a way such that I can call it up this very moment. As knowledge and memory they remain modes of consciousnes and cannot simply disappear like a coin into a gutter in the street. That they are not completely gone is sometimes witnessed to by actions. Thoughts which one has forgotten or, even more so, repressed can have just as great or even greater power than conscious thoughts. For another reason, however, one must assume that repressed thoughts have not fallen completely out of one's consciousness. For how else can it continue to be held in check through repression—where this repression can occur completely subconsciously? The subconscious (in Freud's sense) in general belongs to consciousness as its own underground which is unconscious in a completely different sense than the metabolism processes in the liver. One almost dares to express the paradoxical statement: The unconscious (or subconscious) is a part of the conscious that does not have (at least direct) access to the former. This means more than the statement that one can only say something about one's own subconscious thoughts if they were unconscious and have, since then, become conscious.

183. A third mode of preconscious experience can be added to the second group of modes that was in fact a whole group of modes. It refers to free, moral actions. Most of the time one can only do what one knows to be bad (or evil) if one pretends that it is either not really that bad or necessary or even justified, and so on. Afterward, when one has opened one's eyes and regrets what one has done, one must admit: I knew what I did, or if one does not want to admit

it, one can repress or excuse the action. The positive correlate of this lying-to-oneself is the good action where the right hand does not know what the left hand is doing, that is, in whose excellence the agent is not reflected and does not benefit, although her action cannot be mechanical and must be free and, thus, somehow conscious (see Matthew 5,3f.).

184. A fourth example can be taken from the naive question: Where are thoughts before they come to me? Often thoughts and insights need an incubation period before they are ripe. Occasionally we hope for clarification of a problem by sleeping on it. Our dreams then show—for those who know how to interpret them—that we have "known" something which is still caught up in a picture and has not attained sentential clarity.

The examples can be multiplied, the modes can be distinguished more sharply, the courage—or also the caution—grows in extending the borders for applying the predicate "consciousness." In this context, as it is often the case in this anthropology, what is important is to point to the whole dimension and to sharpen the awareness of the complexity of the matter.

185. What would be the modes of a raised consciousness, a greater awareness, beyond the simple requirement of linguistic formulizability? The awareness of a perception can be raised through an analysis of a relatively vague general impression into its individual parts, through the comprehension of its functional structure, and so on. Knowledge is very useful for these methods. The botanist sees more, the musician hears more and better—assuming that they have acquired their knowledge in the context of seeing and hearing and remain open for the experience of new and particular things that is never just a case of a known generality. Knowledge which one uses in order to elucidate the phenomena can still be an unclear mixture of sentences. Discovering their logical connection, according to the principle of sufficient reason and noncontradiction, means a further increase of consciousness that extends further if one turns

to these principles themselves, being the central lenses in which light is bound together, intrinsic to theoretical consciousness. For the same reason the brightest form of consciousness surpasses itself at this point into darkness: light itself cannot be elucidated through light, but only the non-transparent, the opaque. The more one turns toward it, the more one is blinded (see Aristotle, *Metaphysics* II).

186. Analogies are true for practical knowledge. Whoever sees through a situation will handle it with greater awareness—whoever knows one's own motives—whoever knows more distinctly what one wants—and wants it too. "Aware" and "intentionally" are closely connected. They either are identical ("I am aware of how I am talking" = not accidentally, intentionally) or being together as contrasts ("I am making myself aware of this motive so that it will not be effective in my intentional actions"). In general it seems better to act with awareness than without. This is, however, only true if consciousness remains practical and does not become action-hindering self-consciousness, or hyperreflectivity, that is, to make theoretical the practical consciousness which in effect dissolves it from within. It is true in principle that every light of consciousness is naturally circumscribed by the darkness of the unconscious, a fact that must be accepted if it is to reach the light of consciousness. Once again mere allusions must suffice.

d) Self-consciousness and Consciousness
   of Other Things/Beings

187. A kind of self-consciousness belongs to every form of consciousness of other things/beings, although the former is not, therefore, reducible to the structure of the consciousness of the latter.

In sense perception the perceived object is given to me, but at the same time I am present to myself in a certain way, and the more primitive the dominating sense is, the more "material" the way is. The perception of smells, of spaces,

or of hot/cold is not completed in a merely objective statement, with no relation to myself. If, however, such a statement is made, then it has the character of a certain self-
liberation from the condition of being implied. For the audio
and visual senses this is different. The self-consciousness
that belongs to them has—at least within certain borders
of stimulus intensity—a less physical tone. For this reason
it steps back behind the objective consciousness, whereas
the converse is the case for the "lower" senses. We say "It
feels cold" and "It smells good (to me)" and express foremost mental states, whereas the sentences "A train is coming" and "The siren is sounding" primarily express objective states of affairs, irrespective of the fact that the objective
form of statements can be found in all realms. In the realm
of statements that denote perceptions of the "lower" senses
the subjective affection is already understood along with the
statement, whereas in the field of the higher senses they must
be expressly formulated.

188. At any rate, one discovers oneself not primarily as
the object of perception but rather as its subject: in the mode
of givenness that lies in the bodily feeling of affection or activity; at the same time in the repercussion of an experience
that clouds and colors the mirror of the soul in a certain
way. The formal difference in the mode of givenness has its
influence in the mode of expression. Self-consciousness is
expressed in sentences that begin with "I. . . ." These sentences are not reducible to sentences that begin with the third
person because, in the end, their subjects can only be de-
noted through references (with the finger and such) that must
take their starting point from my, the particular speaker's,
standpoint. Certainly: sentences of the form "I . . ." express
a self-consciousness in the form of objective consciousness.
Thus, it belongs to their meaning that "I" am a person among
other persons about all of whom can be talked objectively.
Nonetheless, "I" is not a context-independent name or in-
dicator for an arbitrary object of discourse. Rather: if there
were no self-consciousness but rather only, or basically only,

objective consciousness, the expressions "I" and "you" would have no meaning other than the expressions "No. A," "No. C," and so on—granted that there could be expressions at all.

189. The content and form of self-consciousness are in a certain way indivisibly connected. I can, either in sequence or almost at the same time, be aware that I am being tickled, that I see the Mississippi in front of me, and that I am neglecting my work. In all of these cases it is always dealing with me. However, the mode of self-consciousness is different, corresponding to the different kinds of states of affairs of which I am aware. A primitive being-at-oneself belongs to a being that is capable of consciouness and self-consciousness, but the concrete forms of self-consciousness that emerge from the correspondence of different life situations and dimensions reveal the richness in content of a personality as well as the differentiation of the formal modes of self-consciousness.

190. Such a basic situation and dimension is the relation to other subjects of self-consciousness. The conviction of the immediate certainty of my own existence, on the one hand, and the question as to the epistemic access to other subjects, on the other hand, have played a large role in modern philosophy of mind. According to Descartes I can be certain of my own existence insofar as it consists in judgmental acts without recurring to the certainty of other beings, especially physical beings to which my own body as well as other persons belong. In this sense, self-consciousness, at least in its core, is divorced from the affirmation of the reality of other conscious beings. Conversely, every certainty regarding others —material things and persons—must be built upon the sole certain basis of self-consciousness. These attempts do not ultimately lead beyond the starting point, as Theunissen (1981) has shown. Compare the parallel position for the problem of one's own body, No. 135, 141, 142. In fact, the sovereign ego-cogito of Descartes cannot get along without the (albeit negative) mediation by the other: in the form of the mediator of tradition whom he has believed up until now and in the form of the hypothetical *genius malignus* (evil

demon) against whose possible attempts at deception it wins a solid place for retreat. Without the resistance of the other the ego would coincide with universal thought and would, thus, lose its individuality and, moreover, reality. It would become merely a function of unity of objective judgments. This individuality is used such that the claim of the existence of other subjects can become a problem in the first place.

Two other problems should not be confused with this one. There is most certainly no intuition of the existence of other subjects that is not mediated through the body, and for this reason one can be mistaken in the interpretation of certain appearances of personality (e.g., see the moving coat and sword figure as a human being, whereas it is in fact only a mechanical puppet). However, in order for me to make a mistake or hit the truth on the mark, I must already have the concept of another person with (and toward) which I interpret the phenomena. It is also granted that it is putting one in another's perspective (empathy) that opens up the other's world, and thus subjectivity (according to which she is an equal and not an object) must be developed and remains often enough minimal. This is still not an argument for the principled priority of self-consciousness over the you-consciousness. For the basic possibility of empathy that one does not want to dispute lives off the accessibility to the other. Of course, I am reliant to a large extent on my own experiences in order to understand the world of another in which lies a limitation in the content of the capacity of empathy.

It is also obvious that I cannot put myself in the other's perspective to such an extent that the personal otherness would disappear and the subjects be interchangeable. However, it does not follow from this that we cannot encounter each other as irreducible persons, as beings which can strain, give, threaten, and help in a way in which only persons can. On the contrary! As was intimated in No. 92-95, we arrive at those modes of self-consciousness in which we cultivate our personal possibilities only through interpersonal mediation, so that the "you" proves to be "older" than the "I" (Nietzsche). We only arrive at the consciousness of our freedom and our personal peculiarity, at the consciousness of our value and, finally, our autonomy in judgment through other's approaching us with these aspects. In this manner the reality of self-consciousness, beyond its mere potentiality in me (that is naturally always to be assumed), depends on the reality of such approaches. It is only when I have become myself that I can become theoretical and relegate the appearing reality to a mere "phenomenon" whose positing of existence must then become the object of an extensive justification.

3. ONTOLOGICAL ASSUMPTIONS OF CONSCIOUSNESS

191. Being itself becomes conscious in consciousness. The movement of becoming conscious belongs for this reason to being just like the hiddenness out of which consciousness emerges and from which it remains enveloped. If the words "truth," "reference," and so on are to have any meaning, one must assume these sentences. What they mean positively remains relatively vague of course, which is to be expected when one is asking about the ground of all clarity. Conversely, what is clear is that its negation destroys the concept of knowledge and its prelevels. Such a negation is present when one defines the concept of being-in-itself through the contrast to the concept of being-for-us, or when one reconstructs the concept of truth purely on the level of converging, coherent, and such opinions and, thereby, drops the element of correspondence with the state of affairs.

Naturally there are not only many degrees of consciousness and knowledge but also various modes of consciousness to which different meanings (and degrees of intensity of these meanings) of being correspond, as would have to be shown in an analysis of historically changing modes of technical, personal, and religious paths of knowledge. The question about the prelevels of consciousness in higher animals would be integrated into this analysis — an immense and immensely difficult task that for this reason cannot be repressed as meaningless. In this context, however, we cannot address this issue at all. Still, the remark is necessary so that one sees that the theme "consciousness" pushes beyond anthropology and into metaphysics — that is, that anthropology leads to metaphysical questions.

Consciousness belongs to being itself. This does not mean that "being" is only what is an object of knowledge or even scientific knowledge — rather that every experience and permeation of being must have its positive possibility in being itself. It also does not mean that being becomes conscious of itself in human (or other finite) consciousness. The motivation for positing such a universal subject is lacking. It does mean, however, that there must be a positive possibility in being itself for a finite subject becoming aware of itself, whether it be in self-consciousness determined in practical life or in transcendental reflection.

192. Transcendental reflection surpasses the conscious (as such) to the conditions of its possibility in the subject. How must the subject be structured in its being such that the manifold layered and differentiated act of identity of consciousness is possible in the subject? Such identity is only possible in particular cases if a membership of our essence in the revealing and concealed being underlies it in principle, and such that this revealing is to be achieved and the concealment endured by us (see Heidegger 1977 and 1969). In our limited perspective, we, as beings capable of consciousness, are associated with being such that "the soul is in a sense all existing things" (Aristotle, *De anima* III,8 431 b21; see No. 29). Not only the individual acts of consciousness and knowledge but also the critical reflections about the truth and adequacy of individual claims and classes of convictions "live" out of this primitive association. The thesis claiming the transience and superficiality of those forms of conscious-

ness that we can secure as knowledge receives its insightfulness from our somehow reaching into the depths of being as well. For otherwise we could never see through the superficial as such.

If these acts of identity are not comprehensible when we attempt to interpret them as material processes (see No. 166–167) and if the self-criticism of the knowing being are outside the scope that is formed by the biological interpretation of truth as utility for life, then the most important categories of understanding through which we attempt to understand our own essence are taken from us. The mystery that attaches to the fact of consciousness and knowledge devolves upon ourselves completely. Since all of what we believe about ourselves in particular cases of knowledge is a form of knowledge and consciousness that, as such, is in its form a secret, all of our empirical knowledge about ourselves remains engulfed by something that is not cognitively alterable anymore, because it makes possible all knowledge. Still, we can at least acknowledge this fact.

II. Freedom of the Will

193. The accessibility of a world in which I encounter human beings, things, and such basically and normally has a practical significance. "World" then means approximately "action situation." In attempting to survive this such and such we are also related to our own life possibilities. Regarding the manner of reaction, different degrees of proximity and distance must be distinguished that exist between the action and the agent—these expressions are initially to be taken very broadly—pure reflex actions (like, e.g., in the knee), instinctive reactions (like, e.g., folding one's arms during an uncomfortable discussion), and deliberate actions (like, e.g., the formulations in a very important letter). It is always I who raises his leg, folds his arms, writes the letter. Still, I as myself am in varying degrees the creator of these activities: my foot moves out, to my surprise; I automatically fold my arms without really wanting to; I have deliberated for a long time what I want to write and acknowledge it as my work. . . . If something proceeds out of myself such that it can in no way be attributed to a cause that only belongs to me as *something of mine* (and, thus, stands in relative otherness to me), then we say that I freely wanted this action.

Not all human actions are freely chosen. If one takes into consideration the totality of our modes of action and the complexity of a single free action, freedom plays perhaps a small, but not the only, role. Without the foundation of reflex reactions, instinctive actions, and other such desires and aversions there would be no free human choices. Still, it is an old conviction that human beings are responsible for their actions, that it is in their power whether they act in such or such a manner—that human agency, where it is specifically human, is structured differently than the reaction of a highly developed primate: due to freedom.

1. THE CONTENT OF THE EXPRESSION "FREEDOM OF THE WILL"

194. In many of the discussions concerning the existence or nonexistence of the freedom of the will this concept of freedom is conflated with others. For this reason our considerations must begin with an exclusion of these related concepts and with a definition of freedom of will.

Originally the word "free" had a social meaning, as a name of a caste. Equal in meaning to "dear" and "cherished"—still today one can speak of a freeman or a free-born citizen—it denotes those who are "dear and cherished" by a speaker belonging to the ruling class: the (more or less related) members at the top of society, the lords or masters. They do what they want, as contrasted with the slaves and others who must do what others want from them. It is from this context that the basic meaning of "freedom" stems: being one's own master, following one's own rules.

a) Different Meanings of "Freedom"

In the following the word "freedom" and "free" shall be used so that it designates the power of an acting subject over certain actions. For our purposes three meanings of "freedom" need to be distinguished.

195. The first is freedom in the sense of arbitrariness, also called "moral freedom": Thus, we may say: "It is up to you whether you park in the garage or not." One who *may* do what one wants, that is, whose *right* to act in this manner

is not limited by moral or judicial *laws,* is free in this sense (regarding certain actions). Freedom of press, religion, coalition, and such belong in this realm.

The second is freedom of action. One is free in this sense (regarding certain actions) if one is *not hindered* from doing what one had planned on doing. Such hindrances might be either inner or outer *constraints.* In this sense a prisoner is not free.

In a society in which the observation of legislative bills is enforced through the application of force (police, penal systems), both forms of freedom or lack thereof move close together in any particular case. In principle, however, their difference remains clear. For there is illegal constraint and unhindered illegality.

196. Being-hindered (or not-being-hindered) and not-being-permitted (or being-permitted) refer to actions that I can and want to execute. A ban or a hindrance regarding an action for which I do not even have the physical, mental, intellectual, and other capabilities draws a blank. Regarding the actions for which I am lacking the capability, the problem of freedom does not arise in any of its meanings, thus also not for freedom of the will. In other words, in the following the word "free" will never be used as in the sentence "I am not free (without the technical means) to fly through the air." A ban is always, a constraint almost always, against actions that someone *wants* to execute. We are distinguishing want from must and desire. Must appears in two different forms, as conditioned and unconditioned. Conditioned must stands in a merely relative contrast to want: "I pay taxes, not because I want to, but because I must" = "I want to pay them in order to avoid a greater misfortune that I do not want to endure." The unconditional must—"He must vomit every time he rides on the bus"—stands in contrast to wanting: What I "must" do lies outside the realm of the power of my will. However, I can desire that I do not feel sick, and I can have the desire of meeting a famous movie star. Desire is a kind of level prior to wanting—a level which

can lead either to wanting or not. Desiring is a playing with different possibilities of striving and of that for which one can strive — a being attracted to and a letting one be attracted to the beautiful, pleasurable, noble, and so on. Without it appearing desirable I cannot want it, but a desire is not a want and a want is more than a mere desire (although in colloquial speech the sentences "I want X" and "I desire X" are often equivalent). For a desire can refer to an impossible object, whether it be impossible in itself (like, e.g., a square circle or a risk-free life of adventure) or impossible for me (like, e.g., being a famous athlete although I am a weakling). A want refers, however, to an action that appears to me to be sensible — as a means to something else or directly — and I must have the capacity for introducing them in my hand. A true want has already proceeded into the realm of action as long as it is not hindered through any compulsion.

197. Wanting has in a sense two sides. On the one hand, it is an active acceptance or rejection of a value. The actual act of wanting, the real choice, occurs in the availability of grasping the value (or what I think it to be) in which I let myself be taken in by the value. On the other hand, it is the automatic bodily transmission of the choice: I stretch out my hand, go on my way, start talking, and so on. "Wanting" is itself not an action, but rather refers to an action. I do not continue having the relationship of control to wanting that is mediated through wanting and that I have to possible actions (or also affections): wanting is an immediate modification of the way in which I act or am affected. "Want" is, like "must," "may," "be," "have," and so on, principally, not an independent verb, but rather an auxiliary or "helping" verb.

b) Freedom of the Will

198. What does the expression "freedom of the will" mean? The capability of, in principle, determining for myself a certain behavior (that is possible for me and judged as

sensible) or repression thereof, respectively, determining this or that behavior, in virtue of the fact that the consciousness of value and the capacity of affirmation are not limited to subjective values but rather open to goodness in an absolute sense. What that means negatively is that the behavior of a free being does not necessarily result in a determinate way from the components of the action situation that are set prior to the choice. Instead of "freedom of will" many say "freedom of choice" (Lat. *liberum arbitrium*), "freedom of determination," and such—there is no unified terminology, as is often the case in philosophy, when new words accompany a new style of thought or old words receive a changed meaning because the subject matter of philosophy is only present in linguistic form and because the truth, despite all absoluteness, is only available in a personal and historical perspective.

199. This—anticipatory—definition is to now be explained via its most important components.

(1) The expression "behavior" was chosen due to its breadth: it encompasses not only activities or actions but also affections, promises, thinking, retention, and so on. In the following we will use the expression "action" in the same broad sense.—The concern is an individual action here and now, not a lasting type of action or behavior (as is most often the case in the use of behavioral psychology).—Does not one choose between things as well (e.g., different soaps from which I want to buy one), and not only between possibilities of action? Certainly, but every choice for a thing is simultaneously a choice about an action (e.g., to buy the soap) that is determined by its object.

(2) Actions possible for me and judged as sensible: only these actions come into question, not simply as something theoretically possible but attractive for me here and now as well as possible (whereby in a situation in which the choice is between two evils the lesser appears comparatively attractive). What is possible for me must also be possible in itself. It must also be sensible for me, that is, it must be judged

or believed to be sensible, whereas it need not be sensible in itself (that is, I might be wrong about what is sensible for me).

(3) The expression "respectively" divides two different kinds of situations of choice and their corresponding mode of freedom: the situation of freedom of execution (*libertas exercitii*) and the situation of freedom of determination (*libertas specificationis*). In the first case one is concerned with either positing or not positing a certain possible action (e.g., to vote for a Democrat or not to vote); in the second case, with positing either this or that action (e.g., to vote for a Democrat or to vote for a Republican). The alternative is different in each case: in the first case the considerations are the reasons for and against X; in the second, the reasons for and against X as well as for and against Y. In the case of freedom of execution I do something that is not X if I decide against X — however, and this is the difference, I have not decided positively what I am doing in place of X. Nevertheless, it is indirectly wanted because it is implicitly accepted. If I enter a situation of choice, there is no way out of the situation anymore. Even the refusal of a real choice is a choice. As finite beings we do not have the choice of whether we enter into situations of choice at all — whether we are free or not.

(4) "Or" designates an alternative: there are at least two real possibilities of acting. As the person who has the alternatives and, thus, the full scope of my judicial choice (*liberum arbitrium*) over its realization I stand above the alternatives. That is the element of power in freedom, but there is also anguish in choices: being torn back and forth between the possibilities which the choice brings to a close. As long as my being stretches along alternative possibilities, I am a living contradiction that pushes toward a solution in favor of one determinately contoured form of action.

(5) In the expression "for oneself" the reciprocity between power and powerlessness can be discovered once more. The expression intimates that the person who decides and the

person about whom something is being decided are one and the same and in the essential unity of activity and passivity.

Activity: in a free choice my deciding is the last cause for my acting such and not otherwise. Of course, I have reasons for acting in such a manner, but these reasons are only in and for the act of deciding. The choice is not the result of internal and external dispositions to act so that the direction of the choice could be set in a determinate way by them. Thus, the choice stands at the beginning of a new state, and for this reason the deciding person (not just some attribute of the person) is the "cause" of the action. Because he is "guilty" of it coming to be such and such and not otherwise, insofar as he could have acted differently, he must be responsible to someone to whom he must account for himself. If he is not capable of entering the process of responsibility or if, within this process, he can deflect his action to something that let the action happen without his involvement, then one will exonerate him from responsibility. For without free will there is no responsibility.

Passivity: Our finitude is effective in that every choice about something comes back to ourselves. In fact, this is true for every action, even those that are not free. Still, there is a kind of repercussion that—according to general consensus—can only come about through free actions. One does not become a "good" or "evil" human being simply through the influence of the surroundings or through heredity which can extensively determine the moral strength of a human being but not infiltrate one's most inner heart. One becomes a good or evil human being through the repercussions of repeated and unexamined good or bad free actions. At any rate, the concepts of the morally good and bad only have meaning with respect to freedom and vice versa. The claim (and denial) of the existence of free will and the objective validity of moral values go hand in hand.

(6) "In principle" means the capacity of self-determination. That means making a difference between the different de-

grees of readiness a capacity has for a free choice, in which the one builds on the other. The basic capacity for self-determination in the horizon of the idea of a truly meaningful life, peculiar to all human beings as such, must mature in order to become an effective capacity in the depth of its comprehension. In this sense we deny a very small child the effective capacity for free self-determination, although it has the "equipment" for it and is approached with regard to developing it. Even the actions of adults are not always free, and among the free ones there are varying degrees, each according to the degree of knowledge of the difference in values and the real circumstances of the choice—each according to the degree of internal independence from the pressure of one's desires and surroundings—in short, all of those factors that, for example, can be counted as mitigating or aggravating circumstances in court.

200. Freedom as arbitrariness and freedom of action were definable through the absence of a limiting factor, as prohibition or force; these factors work against free actions that are already in the process of becoming realized. The freedom of will has its contrast in the fact that the act is partially or completely determined by its assumptions prior to all free choice. If it is partial, then there remains a margin for possibilities that can be larger or smaller, but at any rate limited. If it is complete, then there is no room at all for the freedom of will. For this reason one calls philosophers who deny the existence of the freedom of will (for human beings) "determinists." Although free determination is a mode of determination, one neglects this linguistic usage and intends the complete determination of action that excludes freedom. When we speak of determinism and of the determinists in the following, we will use the word in its narrow meaning. Thus, whoever claims that there is also determination of natural necessity is not to be called a determinist. Where we talk of "freedom" in the following without any further specification, we will always mean freedom of the will.

2. POSITIVE EXHIBITION OF THE EXISTENCE OF FREEDOM

201. Until now we have limited ourselves to developing a concept of freedom from our general everyday experiences and convictions. Now, however, the determinists are denying the real validity of this concept, thus, the existence of freedom of will. In this manner Spinoza (*Ethics* II, Theorem 35, note) claims that human beings think they are free because they are aware of their inclinations and not the causes for them. Lévi-Strauss (1975, 737) thinks that it is an essential feature of agency consciousness to lie to oneself, following Nietzsche's phrase of the "attitude of pious illusion in which alone all that wants to live can live" (*On the Advantage and Disadvantage of History for Life,* No. 7). Today we are very sensitive about such disclosures of pitfalls and hidden difficulties. The mentioned positions certainly have their element of truth. The question for us is, however, whether that element of truth excludes the freedom of will.

We must expressly defend the validity of our analysis against the deterministic denial of the existence of freedom. This can occur such that we either prove our own claim or critically refute the arguments of the opposing side. We will attempt both, the positive exhibition in this section, the negative one in the third and fourth sections.

a) Exhibition from the Contradiction of Two Assumptions

202. The concept of responsibility is necessarily tied to the concept of freedom of will. Without the real validity of the former, any blame or praise in the moral realm, as Aristotle has already shown (*Nichomachean Ethics,* III, 7), is without any objective foundation.

If one denies the reality of freedom in principle and, at the same time, expresses moral judgments on others or oneself or makes moral demands, then one has made two contradicting claims. In order to avoid the contradiction, one must rescind one of the theses.

203. The determinist will attempt to hold onto determinism and to let go of those activities and views that imply the claim of freedom. Since, however, it is not a merely theoretical claim but rather is concerned with life-implying convictions, this reform does not proceed without extreme measures of self-constraint and a theoretical mastering of the unalterable "archaic" remains of theory-contradicting actions. This process of reform is certainly very useful. For much too often our thirst for revenge and our need for a scapegoat assume full responsibility and, thus, freedom, whereas responsibility and freedom are present either not at all or to a reduced extent if considered more closely and soberly. Because an action contradicts an ideal of action, we tend to punish the transgressor of this ideal, whether it be ourselves or others, without having checked whether the person made responsible was even capable of achieving the ideal. (A separate question which cannot be discussed here is the justification and especially the structure of the judicial penal system. It should only be noted that the therapeutical and socializing measures, insofar as they are instituted under constraint, are justified and must be rationally acceptable for the person being punished.)

Finally, the Gospel (Matthew 7, 1-5) says, "Do not judge, that you may not be judged." However, this formulation condemns judgment as a vehicle of—often hypocritical—self-righteousness and injustice, but not all judgment. Could the living otherwise be told of the coming judgment? Additionally, the imperative would be senseless if one could not freely take heed of it. As far as transferring responsibility to a scapegoat is concerned, this transferal assumes a recognition of, but not an acknowledgment of, the responsibility that is to be transferred. It is very difficult or impossible to be completely successful at liberating oneself from the lust for revenge and the tendency of placing oneself over another in condemnation—to free oneself from the hopeful belief in free choice in the face of the truly good is impossible as long as one still has human sensations.

b) Exhibition from the Contradiction of Statement and Positing

204. The situation of the discussion in this case is such that the determinist does not claim two claims that do not agree with each other but rather just the one claim that there is no freedom of will. We will now try to show that every claim — thus, the determinist's as well — lives off the conviction that the person who claims as well as the addressee of the claim are free with regard to their claims. Thus, we would have a contradiction between the sentence that is being claimed and the conviction that every positing of claims assumes.

205. Any claim necessarily implies the assumption that its content corresponds to the truth, and that this being true is clear to the person making the claim: that she has consciously discarded other possible claims in favor of the one that appears to her to be true and that she has given up the possibility of taking something useful or pleasurable as the criterion of her choice in favor of truthfulness. This state of affairs fulfills the concept that we have created concerning a free choice. The suspicion (that may very well be founded in a particular case, as in the case of a certain lasting or temporary mental illness) that, in principle, a mechanism of true agency conceals itself underneath such a choice and lets the phenomenon of choice appear as an illusion is not only unfounded but also destroys the minimal concept of knowledge without which the sharpest skeptic cannot survive.

The same result arises from the expectations that any participant in a discussion has of his partner. He will not be content if I simply outwardly accept his opinion in order to do him a favor. He will also decline the eventual possibility of conditioning me physiologically or psychologically so that

I only express deterministic statements. He wants me to choose freely and wholeheartedly, in the light of several possible statements, the one which appears to be true to me — and hopes that this is the same as he holds to be true.

206. If in the limited field of a discussion about theories freedom of will is admitted, then the universality of the deterministic thesis is broken. Moreover, there is no reason anymore to limit the realm of freedom to choices between statements and to postulate the sole rule of deterministic mechanisms in the practical realm. For the human being who is inquisitive will battle with emotional and other fixations. Taking a position on possible statements is also a kind of praxis (action) within the horizon of truth that is the specific "good" of the understanding. Finally, it is not only inner knowledge but also linguistic apparatus that (normally) listens to my will by transmitting the truly known — certainly with the help of the "mechanics" of the linguistic centers, lungs, vocal cords, and so on, but not "mechanically." In affirming and denying judgments "a willful taking of a position or an alternative behavior to the value is present, and it is exactly in *this* point, . . . that the other valuing behavior of the subject is similar to it" (Rickert 1921, 303).

c) Theoretical and Practical Certainty

207. After one has understood what the expression "freedom of will" means and realized what one assumes when one discusses an issue objectively, one cannot seriously claim that we are not free. Any possibly theoretically conceivable form of determinism is opposed to the factual conviction of freedom. The demonstration of this consists in the fact that the view from the level of conceivable or establishable facts is reduced in kind to the level of things experienced and affirmed by me. One could object that in principle only a conviction has been exhibited with regard to which the determinist must also admit that he shares it in practice — but not the (in a sense "naked") existence of freedom itself. What

can appear as a criticism is, however, just a consequence of the peculiarity of freedom, in existence and "givenness." For the existence of freedom is not primarily the object of a neutral establishing but rather becomes accessible from the life praxis for this life praxis, in the experience of the reciprocity of having to decide and hope. A certain element of trust and hope cannot be crossed out due to the mode in which freedom becomes accessible—to ourselves and others. For this reason the proof of freedom does not lead to a "pure" fact such that the "right" of the action guiding conviction could then be tested from this standpoint. Still, since the doubt about freedom proves to be something that assumes the conviction of the effective freedom of judgmental assent, one cannot distance oneself from the stubbornness of the belief in freedom that accompanies agency consciousness in the same way that one can distance oneself to a certain extent from the prejudices of one's epoch. There is no reason to assume such a deep self-deception in our essence—except for the reasons given in support of the deterministic thesis. How it accords with these we will shortly see, and it will be shown that it would be wrong to talk of clear evidence for determinism.

208. Of course, one can be deceived in any particular case in one's assessment of one's own and others' actions as free, but this answers the question whether the idea of an action brought forth by a free choice can be attributed to this particular action here and now, and not the question whether this idea of freedom is in principle fantastical or realistic. Such deceptions are uncovered when a manifest determination (e.g., through transition mechanisms or posthypnotic commands) turns out to be a cause for the action thought to be free. A criterion for the positive participation of the subject cannot be as clearly stated as the negative ones. For we have, not an intellectual intuition of the existence of freedom for knowledge, but rather only an indirect consciousness of the same, directed essentially toward action, that is implied in the practical consciousness of true evaluative al-

ternatives. Whoever is still suspicious of this mode of given-ness and demands a more geometrical kind of proof turns out to be someone who does not have sufficient knowledge of the matter to know what is capable or in need of a proof and what not, and if so, what kind of proof is necessary (see Aristotle, *Nichomachean Ethics* I,1 1094 b23).

209. With respect to the freedom of individual actions, objectified through reflection or observation, we can be deceived. One can also be deceived in the theoretical interpretation of freedom. Still, there is no necessity present forcing us to deny the possibility of free actions, but such a necessity is claimed if the thesis of determinism can be shown to be true. In the following we will examine the reasons that determinists give for their claim. Two aspects of the one freedom, in the form of two denials, diverge, which should be apparent in the section coming to a close: the indeterminateness of the agent as the origin (*causa efficiens*) of the agent's actions, and the unlimitedness of the motivational horizon (the *causa finalis*) of the agent's actions. Correspondingly, mechanistic (3) and teleological (4) determinism are to be dealt with.

3. LACK OF REASONS FOR MECHANISTIC DETERMINISM

210. Under "determinism" we mean, not the claim that human agency also stands under mechanical and teleological determinations (so-called "soft" determinism), but that it stands *exclusively* under such determinations (so-called "hard" or proper determinism).

The classical formulation of mechanical determination was given by the astronomer Pierre Simon Laplace (d. 1827): "If we know the state of the universe at time t as well as all of the laws of nature, we can derive the state of the universe at any time earlier or later than t," whereby the possibility, in principle, of knowing the first two is assumed because the events themselves are so deterministically structured that an image of these structures in knowledge of the described kind is possible.

211. It is clear that the claim of freedom and the deterministic claim cannot subsist together. Nevertheless, we have an interest in both of these theses. This interest is distinguished in its kind from the interest in determinism that one has who wants to get out of taking responsibility and from the interest in the claim of freedom that one has who wants to live out his lust for revenge on the guilty party. It is rather an interest of reason that combines us with both of these theses (see Kant, *Critique of Pure Reason*, B 471–480, 560–586): We want to hold onto freedom because it is the prerequisite for practical and theoretical judgment. We want to hold onto universal necessity because natural science and technology appear to rely on it. The most simple measure of commonsense knowledge, unalterable for life, would be ruined in the triviality of a mere chance natural event.

*a) Incommensurability of Freedom and
Complete Determination*

Since we have such a fundamental interest in both of the contrary claims, it seems provident to see whether the contradiction is perhaps just an apparent one. Two such theories will be briefly sketched and checked, that of Moore and that of Kant.

212. George Edward Moore offers an interpretation in his *Principia ethica* (1903) of the expression "He could have acted otherwise" with which the freedom of the action is expressed. This formulation, according to him, means "Something else could have happened—since all of the circumstances of the situation are purely contingent states of affairs." If the circumstances, the prior history of the agent, or the consciousness of the consequences relevant to the action had been different, the agent would have acted differently—irrespective of the fact that the action, as it took place, was

the necessary consequence of the internal and external circumstances (see Ricken 1977, Pothast 1978, 142-156). In this manner freedom and determinism are conjoined. In fact, however, this is illusory. For freedom was sacrificed to determinism. The general contingence of the prior conditions of every action does not ground freedom. For this it is necessary that the action itself results contingently out of the prior conditions. The could-have-happened-differently that is attributed to the free subject is more and different than the mere "It is possible that he acts such, or also otherwise" (see Tugendhat 1986, 194–197).

213. Immanuel Kant believed to be able to combine a complete natural determinism with freedom of the will by dividing free autonomy into a purely intellectual (noumenal) realm, not accessible to our knowledge, and necessity into the realm of the sense-objective appearing reality. Every action can then be traced back to its natural causes as well as to free choice without the one excluding the other (*Critique of Pure Reason* B 561–586; see Carnois 1973, Beck 1960, 176–208). However, on the level of the phenomena (if "phenomena" has not already been narrowed) we normally distinguish between a free and an unfree action as well as an action from an event, even though it is difficult to determine in particular cases. There are mitigating and excusing circumstances. Kant's radical separation of the phenomenal from the noumenal does not seem to take this into account. A freedom that is effective in worldly actions is only possible if the world is not completely deterministically structured according to the closed Newtonian system.

214. Both of the attempts at combining freedom of the will and complete natural determination have not succeeded. The same can be said of other attempts in the same direction (see Pothast 1980, 125-175). Although it cannot be excluded that further combination models will be conceived of, there is nothing in favor of a high probability for their success. Thus, it seems prudent to look more closely at the reasons that are given in favor of the deterministic claim to

see whether one is forced either to combine freedom and determinism or to sacrifice freedom to determinism.

b) The Impossibility of Proving Determinism

215. The reasoning for determinism could be attempted, stated roughly, in three ways, inductively, deductively, or reductively.

The inductive empirical method of proof founders on the peculiarity of the statement to be proved, namely, complete generality and necessity. Such sentences can only be proven deductively. But from which premises? Disregarding that determinists generally loath metaphysical argumentation to which, however, in this case they would have to recur, it is difficult to derive the deterministic causality principle from a more general one. The sentence "Every contingent existence requires a cause," whose interpretation and grounding has its own problems, does not suffice to exclude free causes.

216. Thus, only reductive arguments remain: One interprets the deterministic principle as an hypothesis for which there are no further grounds and which is responsible for the explanation of natural processes and justified by its fruition. Its generality is that of a program that is confirmed to the degree that one is successful in carrying it out. To present the totality of causes and effects — the explanations and predictions — that refer to a particular event remains an idea that motivates research, whereas it remains an open question as to what extent this idea matches the basic structure of reality in itself. That such a match cannot be assumed a priori results from the failure of the attempts to interpret the quantum-physicalistic indeterminism in such a way that the indeterminacy lies on the side of ascertainability and not also in reality (see Büchel 1965, 400–425, Heisenberg 1962). In fact, natural laws are the expression, not of an essential relation, but rather of a very large statistical probability. In psychology, which is of special relevance for our problem, one can often only speak of a certain probability. However,

even a large statistical probability for a certain action in a certain situation does not exclude that the individual "expected" action could have proceeded out of a free choice. Thus, the claim that the deterministic principle is a principle of reality in itself drops as an unjustified, uncritical ontologizing claim.

c) Reciprocity of Freedom and Determinism in an Action

217. There is no utterly free self-determination without the coeffects of natural determination in human life. For this reason the natural determination of human actions must be thought of, conversely, as open to possible self-determination. This openness can only be interpreted from the fact and meaning of freedom; the exhibition of the weak reasons for universal determinism only shows the nonimpossibility of freedom, not its reality, and thus not the positive openness of "nature" to freedom. Such openness is to be established in two ways: in one way, freedom and necessity belong together like dialectic counterparts, in the other way, like a foundation and superstructure.

218. The following is meant by dialectic reciprocity: as we have shown above (No. 204–206), the knowledge and claim of objective determinism assumes the freedom of the epistemic and claiming subject. The growing building of known lawlike regularities is, thus, a witness to the freedom of the human mind. At the same time, every new discovery of a lawlike connection is the first step in the extension of the practical elbowroom for actions and, thus, of the effective alternatives of choices. The acknowledged necessity is, therefore, the product as well as an assumption of free activity. The necessity does not become merely subjectively imagined for this reason. It is only when the concern is objective necessity that a reliable knowledge of it and a free planning of technical introduction is possible. Otherwise, science would be a chance game of impressions, and technology a hazardous game. Freedom and natural necessity

are, in their contrast, in solidarity with one another. This is true not only for the realm of knowledge of and control over nature but, in a different way and to a lesser degree, also in the realm of interpersonal relations. The openness for the novel, underivable, and so on must also be present in this latter realm, that is, there must be present the openness of giving freedom, as well as others with their freedom, some space. However, we can only achieve such openness if the actions of others occur according to familiar patterns, laws, and such in most areas, so that I can approximate the reactions of others to my initiatives. A society of purely unpredictable human beings would not be a garden of freedom. It is only the *total* calculability of the actions of cohuman beings, not an extensive calculability, that stands in contrast to their freedom.

219. This brings us to the other relation between freedom and necessity which can be interpreted according to the schema of foundation and superstructure. The human being does not emerge through her free will. According to her first mode of existence she is the product of a very determinate world and developmental process whose direction could have run differently, whose partial processes, however, had to have occurred during the last 20 billion years as they did in order to prepare the way for free choice (see Breuer 1983). This history is not just the past but is in its result lasting present. Only in a certain arrangement of the solar system do the conditions for earthly life remain intact; only when the metabolism of the human organism functions properly, only when the unconscious processes sustaining the soul's life are essentially in order, can the wonder of freedom occur. Still, freedom cannot be reduced to any law of the mentioned arrangement. Without the wisdom of the body the wisdom of the human mind could not develop. Without the spontaneity of desires and movement the idea of a free self-determination would be up in the air. Only a subject that is already determined as a subject can continue to be self-determining, but it is determined such that not

everything is already present and ready, but rather that this determinateness occurs as an assumption and moment of self-determination.

220. Natural determinations that lie prior to actions such that they make them possible (or *per accidens* impossible) are epistemically accessible from there. Most of the time the occasion is negative: that such conditions are normally satisfied can be seen when one searches for the cause of the malfunctioning of the capacity for free self-determination. Normal interpersonal contact with a human being who is obviously not in control of himself has been disrupted. Such a partner must be viewed as a machine that is temporarily out of order. If the disturbance can be corrected with physiological methods that rely on the recognition of the fact that the action of this human being stands under natural laws, the healed patient will be treated, not as an apparatus that works once again, but rather like a free partner—different from a repaired chess computer.

The explanation of human actions as a whole according to natural laws has a place on the edge of true interpersonal exchange that does not yet, not anymore, or only halfway work in the transition from the passive to the technological reference to reality. To claim mechanical determinism as the basic law of all movement thus means: to declare the technological attitude to be the sole legitimate and objectively correct attitude—or else it means nothing practically relevant. In itself the structure of natural processes of which cosmology speaks is prior, but this priority is just a beginning: the available beginning for something in which it is elevated, conserved, and abolished in a higher and more comprehensive order, the negatively necessary basics of free self-determination in the horizon of the good (see Scheler 1957, 164). "Reasons" are not reducible to "causes," belonging to totally different contexts of thinking and action. Causes belong to the context of explaining natural phenomena, whereas reasons have their place in practical reasoning, that is, the planning of my own future actions and the comprehension of past actions, especially of other people. Interpreting by principle every "reason" as being just the covered representer of some natural cause is equivalent to reducing the world of human reasoning and action to the world of natural events. This is a category mistake. Further: We have to reflect on the fact that the world of natural events, insofar as it is reconstructed by science by means of concepts like "cause," is part of the world of human reasoning. Thus we see that it would be nonsense to reduce the meaning of "reason" to "cause,"—as it would be equally nonsense to do it the other way round (see Beck 1975).

4. THE LACK OF REASONS FOR TELEOLOGICAL DETERMINISM

221. Mechanistic determinism denies any spontaneous emergence, thus, any subjectivity. Teleological determinism lies within the realm of subjectivity, that is, goal-directed action, but assumes that the realm of goals is determinately set by the desire structure of the agent—by the particular desire structure of the individual and the desire structure of the living organism "human being" whose basic laws are given in survival and reproduction of the species and/or the attainment of pleasure. If a human being asks himself how he should act, then, speaking with Schopenhauer (*Collected Works,* I München 1911, 179), the vital basic drive turns on a light in order to better grasp the conditions of the realization of his wants. Reasonable deliberation refers only "instrumentally" to the methods of realization, not to the evaluation of whether the goals are valued enough to be realized.

a) The Standard of Practical Deliberation

222. It remains to be shown that the human being is capable of knowing and affirming the intrinsically good that is not relative to her desire dynamics. The core of her free-

dom lies in this capacity. Highly developed animals also have a certain capability for deliberation and choice. They can weigh risks, advantages and disadvantages, and come to a "reasonable" solution. Of course, the realm of experience and especially fantasy-based anticipation extend much further in human beings. Human beings also have more precise instruments of deliberation and a more comprehensive arsenal of available techniques of all kinds. However, a human being's freedom in the face of the possible courses of action would only be greater in degree than that of animals to whom we do not bestow responsibility, and not in principle, if the former's choice did not stand on a different horizon of goodness—namely, on the horizon of the simply good, of the sensible in itself. The human being is free with respect to the manifold relative goods through this reference.

Every value-laden alternative can only appear in a common horizon. Otherwise there would be no basis for comparison and, thus, no alternative. The common horizon is the standard for the evaluation of the value (of goodness) of alternative actions, that is, their objects. In its light they appear as partially good, partially not. Taking a banal example of choosing between foods, the one proves to be good, the other as less good or bad, measured by the standard of taste, agreeability, price, whether it be within one of the standards or within the horizon that arises in a combination of standards. In order to be able to weigh particular concrete goods and to be free toward them, I must have already—either consciously or naively—bound myself to a higher standard.

223. Now I can formulate my standards myself and undergo critical scrutiny and evaluation—with respect to a certain situation of choice or with respect to all possible action situations of a certain kind (for example, today—or forever—the standard of taste is to be the highest!). Such a choice between standards naturally needs a higher standard (in the example above: the pleasure that can be found more in a balanced middle, being considerate to my stomach and

wallet, or more in peak experiences). These standards can be distanced as well, like the principle "pleasure" and the principle "help for suffering." What standard is underlying in this case? The standard is so general and comprehensive that the concern is not any particular kind of good but simply the Idea of the Good. That the human being is capable of raising herself up to this standard containing the good not merely as functionality or as a quality of experience but rather in itself constitutes her freedom. What is intended is not a necessarily conscious, nor a merely theoretically enduring, lift, but rather a practical one that is given when one finds oneself in front of alternatives whose difference in values is such that the absolute, ultimate horizon has been uncovered. This is the case every time one of the exclusive alternatives bears moral character.

The moral value has its peculiarity in that it demands its realization unconditionally. It presents itself as the here-and-now, absolute Good that is not relative to my desires. Still, there arises out of my factual desiring an idea of the good that is independent of the moral good. The desire pushes for its fulfillment; the moral demand, for its realization; I am standing in the middle and can choose because neither one of the goods combines all goodness in itself at which I am aiming.

b) Freedom for the Good

224. The idea of the simply good, that is, the good not only relative to egocentric desires, and thus the idea of freedom depend on the objectivity of moral value and on the possibility of affirming something good in itself for its own sake. That there is something like objective moral values is a topic for discussion concerning the foundation of ethics. Here the accent is to be placed on the second question, the enabling of the subject for the good for its own sake.

225. Kant distinguishes (in the *Foundations to the Metaphysics of Morals,* II. Section) subjective standards ("max-

ims") of my actions that I have, in fact, made my own either consciously or through naively adopting others' and objective standards that say what the principle of an action should be ("imperatives" seen grammatically). Imperatives that one commands of another are of two forms: hypothetical ("*If* you want x, *then* you must also want y!') and categorical ("Want y!"). An hypothetical (conditioned) imperative appeals to a will that is already present in me and shows me, by referring to natural laws, the path to its consequent realization. It has the form of technical instructions and prescriptions in the widest sense. The form of moral instructions is the categorical (unconditioned) imperative. It demands that I want something determinate. What support do I have, how can I make it my own maxim?

The principle upon which the claim of whoever is making the demand is supported can be power. He promises a reward or threatens suffering. The anchoring place in me for such a demand is fear and desire, in short: my neediness. The means to its satisfaction are possessed by the other. However, an imperative supported in such a manner is already hypothetical. One understands how it is effective but not how its power justifies a right to be subjected. One sees that the acceptance of such a threat or promise is not a morally motivated action. Rather, if there are moral demands at all, then they are justified through the inner value of what the concern is — through the immanently valued existence of a human being, for example, that is to be respected — not through an appeal to my factual interest or to our common factual interests. The moral imperative, on the one hand, speaks unconditionally and cannot be bartered with. On the other hand, it speaks defenselessly: because it can only be accepted, without any reserves, freely and when it is listened to in its original meaning. The hypothetical imperative works, ultimately, with the chains that bind us to our neediness. The categorical has, as its sole ally, our insight into the objectively good.

Of course, in all human societies sanctions are connected

with obedience and disobedience toward the moral norms (as with all other norms) since moral motivation alone (for most humans or, in general, most of the time) is not strong enough to guarantee the socially useful and necessary respectable actions. One must, on the one hand, guard oneself against declaring such sanctions (also for oneself) to be unnecessary or immoral; on the other hand, the view toward the sanctions alone can justify neither the morality of an action nor the moral value of following a legitimate demand. In a demand that proceeds from the objectively good the subject recognizes a demand that it directs inside to itself because freedom and the aim toward what is good in itself are identical. The truly good is the inner law of freedom.

226. Is this inner law something other than the internalized form of the norms recognized in my society (family, group, etc.)? The part of social psychology that studies the mechanisms of such internalization seems to be giving, *prima facie,* an explanation of the putative free and selfless actions from egocentric and irresistible motivations. The small child has a strong impulse in itself to imitate what is strongly encouraged by its parents. The bundle of impulsive desires of which the mental apparatus of a child consists to a large extent sets up a border for this natural tendency and obedience to its parents that can only be pushed back by the representation of special rewards and special punishment, that is, through the mobilization of even more powerful desires and fears. In the extreme case little Johnny sees his manhood or life threatened. He flees from the unbearable tension between the impulsive desires and the fear that is connected with the ban: he identifies with the threatening instance, the father as the representative of the commands, so that the previously external instance becomes a mental instance of the superego. The childish ego thus gains a similar power over its id as the father has over it. The substance of the superego and of the relative superiority given by it over the claims of the impulses is, however, itself desire based: it is fear. The unconsciously arising fear of the punishing legislator provides

the energy for the relinquishment of impulses that is constantly asked for by the moral law.

227. What is explained here, and what not? Without a doubt this theory, stemming from S. Freud, illuminates the emergence of moral convictions in an, at first, "innocent" amoral human child that only follows its desires because it is at the mercy of them. This theory is also very helpful in the question as to what a compulsive or scrupulous conscience is or how it comes to be. Thus, this theory also gives a clue as to how to distinguish the free and objectively proper conscientious judgment from the statement of a "conformity" conscience formed out of fear, or at least it is a start in the right direction. The uncovering of the compulsive identification mechanisms that can lead to a hindrance of free-ego development does not have the intention of pressing human beings into mere compulsive beings but rather wants to liberate, through the recognition of the psychological natural laws, from a dominance of the compulsive factors in a realm in which they do not centrally belong.

Of course, psychic determinants play a large role in the development of the ego, in good and bad — and an upbringing or a therapy that means well but does not have a conscious or unconscious objective understanding can fail due to it. The converse is true as well: when the weak ego does not receive any selfless attention from the parents and therapeutical people and is not approached in its capability to live with real values due to insight, it cannot develop and remains under the dominance of the id and the superego, of desire and fear. The weak ego, for example, cannot liquidate its Oedipus complex because the father has not solved his Laios complex, that is, his selfish identification with the son through which, on the one hand, the son is the continuation of himself and, on the other hand, the rival successor. The hate toward the other ego as a shadow follows the love to the second ego. A strong superego can emerge out of such a constellation, but not a free subject. Freedom only develops out of selfless sympathy, out of freedom.

Analytical developmental and social psychology, thus, sharpen the awareness for the peculiarity of a truly moral attitude rather than annihilating it if it can free itself from certain dogmatic assumptions which Freud held onto coming from his background in physiology. That this true morality is not to be confused with the "moral" which one refers to in order to turn one's life fear into gold or to oppress others is an old insight newly discovered and reasoned for by depth psychology. The same is true for the insight that no one can simply jump over her psychological conditions by decree. She can work on it through the techniques of self-conditioning and, thus, extend the limits of her freedom that have normally remained within a certain range (see Grom 1982), although under the conditions that were mentioned in No. 239-240.

c) The Meaning of Freedom

228. Why are we free at all, why must we carry the burden of choice and responsibility? If freedom only referred to the choice of the means for realizing an existential goal implanted in us of which we could not, in turn, make any intrinsic sense, the question would remain unanswered. Such conceivable goals could be: the survival of one's own life and the transmittance thereof to the siblings, the pleasurable feelings of happiness and good luck, the utility for a larger whole. Are they meaningful? Not without further ado, and for this reason we can refuse these goals for ourselves, that is, we have a choice between them, so that they cannot be the last natural horizon of all choices. We hang onto meaningful life and the desire to pass it on. Whoever finds life meaningless prefers death and would not unreasonably demand of his siblings that they carry the burden of a meaningless life. What makes life meaningful? That one is useful for something, and only when this something is meaningful in itself and not just useful or even senseless, and if one is not simply used but rather is freely available.

Of course, it must also be fun in a sense. To what extent does fun or pleasure make life meaningful? The mere avoidance of great displeasure — that one can live life without too much difficulty and displeasure — is certainly not enough. There must really be joy and fun. The enjoyment of the senses is an important component. This, however, cannot be enough for a mortal being who wants to know why one is here. He wants not only to have pleasure but also to be recognized and accepted and be capable of giving out recognition and acceptance. What is missing in this realm one often tries to compensate for — and unsuccessfully at that — by forced, excessively sought-after sensual satisfaction, up to an addiction. This fact indirectly proves that the peculiarly human lack of moderation with regard to his desires is not merely a natural data but rather the result of a sensualization of his infinite mental striving. The countertest consists in the experience that human beings can tolerate very much frustration and pain if they only know the reason for it. A certain, exceedingly variable measure of natural sensual pleasure belongs to the feeling of living a fulfilled life. The proper meaning, however, consists in the affirming act of what can only be freely affirmed: goodness that is immanently being as such. Out of such a selfless affirmation grows a self-realization whose fruit is joy, the purest form of pleasure.

Beyond all special forms of the good the human striving capacity, the will, is not limited to goodness in its absoluteness. For this reason it is free for the particular goods. The meaning of freedom — on its way to itself — must lie in finding good in the concrete that is deserving of being unconditionally affirmed, and that coincides in a sense with the natural affirmation of the good in general that our basic will continually executes.

D. The Unity of Human Existence and the Question as to Its Meaning

229. The starting point of our anthropological path was the desire to know who we really are insofar as we are human beings. For the sake of the objectivity of the sought-after knowledge detours had to be made. Thus, we came back to ourselves from the distant foreignness of being an animal among other animals (Part A). In a middle position the form of our self-relation was settled, and it resulted in the interpretation of our worldly existence as to its basic dimensions (Part B). In the thematization of being able to have knowledge and of our freedom (Part C) we caught up with the starting point of our question: the desire for self-knowledge and trust in its possibility. Thus, the description of our existence is essentially finished, although it may have remained fragmentary in many places.

230. The leading idea of our interpretation was the idea of subjectivity, or of our self-relation, whereby this latter expression points toward a relation to a relation that is related to itself (see No. 154). Both parts of this formula are related

to one another. Neither does the first exist without the second, nor the second without the first, although they have very diverse characters. The first and fundamental relation is the one which humans share in some way with the (higher) animals (see No. 28 and 30). The second relation is bound up with the first one: it consists in the fact that we not only live in relations, but that we live these relations — and so ourselves — in a mediate way, by means of conscience and free choice. Without the first type of relation there would be no reality to live; without the second our way of life would not be different from animal life. This implies that the two relations are not just superimposed, but that they interpenetrate each other so that one human life results. Relational human life is one reality, internally so differentiated, that — in abstract language — it makes sense to isolate two types of constitutive relations. In self-consciousness the human being becomes aware of herself as a bodily desiring being — but such that this self-consciousness does not merely have her conscious thought as an object outside herself, but rather such that it modifies the mode of bodily desires. Without the first relation the second would have no content; without the second the first would have no human form. Therefore, human existence has a twofold character: on the one hand, a transcendence via knowledge and freedom beyond the mere factual (thus a refutation of all reductionisms!) — and, on the other hand, the boundness of the transcending to a certain body, situation, and so on, that is crossed over as well as taken into possession by the transcending.

This twofold relation is constitutive for the existence of the human being. It is his substantiality. A substance is an existing being that stands in itself and as such has a kind of permanence and internal unity. These features are all the more present in a being that also shows features that are characteristic for subjectivity (see No. 27-31). The substance that is characterized by this twofold relation — that is, that has its independence in the ontological liveliness of the being-outside-of-oneself and being-at-oneself — is called a person (see Lotz 1967, 372–402; Müller 1971, 83–122; Theunissen 1966). The ontological meaning of "person" has been influenced by Boethius (*De duabis naturis,* no. 3) with respect to a terminological grasping of the problems of Christology and the Trinity. He defines the person as the indivisible carrier of a spiritual being (*naturae rationalis individua substantia*). In this use of the word its basic meaning is only retained in traces: to be the respective "mask" of a speaker that can speak in his role as mayor, then as the father of his family, then as the authorized representative of his boss. This is much more true of the further development of the concept in which the meaning increasingly converges to the described ontological nature insofar as this is a reason for immediate rights and duties.

231. A sketch of the structure of human existence does not exhaust the intent of our question that underlies the search for an understanding of our essence. For why should we want to know who or what we really are? This knowledge is not meaningful wholly in itself. In its intent it is not the repose of a theoretical view in the known that as such has already allowed the highest fulfillment. Rather, the search for that knowledge and, accordingly, the knowledge itself have a centrally practical component—not in the sense of pragmatic, but in the sense of life orientation. The anthropological search, up to its palaeontological and ethnological branches, receives its dynamics from the search for a possibility of bestowing onto this life our having a livable meaning and, in tendency at least, a comprehensive meaning for the whole.

The meaning of life—in particular life situations as in the whole of life—is something that we are *searching* for—thus, something that is already there in a sense and must only be found. However, we can only search for and find this meaning in such a manner that we experiment with ourselves as an entrance and open and bind ourselves to what turns out (through its inner coherence) to be binding.

232. This is a search for every human being, and that

to the extent that she is forced to it by her nature, history, and capacity for it. Due to the great diversity of fates in life and due to the essentially practical nature of grasping this meaning, a general anthropological science and reflection is beyond the scope of such a search. It cannot take over from each individual his searching, mistakes, and discovery by giving reliable theoretical information and practical routes. What can be given, however, is a kind of dialectic typology of strategies as to how to be directed toward a comprehensive meaning of life. Without being either able or permitted to anticipate how meaningful life can or must look for each individual, certain, especially negative, laws can be formulated under which the search for meaning is carried out.

In the following paragraphs something should be said about the basic tension in human existence from which the question for meaning arises as well as about attempts to answer this question in a way that the basic tension is avoided (I). Then, the concern is to point out a direction in which an appropriate answer must lie (II). Finally, something must be said about the relationship between philosophical anthropology and theology (III).

I. The Basic Tension in Human Existence

The form of existence that is characterized by *every* subjectivity (see No. 28 and 30) is something laden with tension: always threatened, always to be taken in the right dosage, never to be brought into a peaceful state prior to the end, death. Through the relation to the relation (see No. 154 and 230) that characterizes the free and conscious form of existence a new tension arises, namely, that between what sways freely in the relationship *to* the relationship and the comparatively stable part of the basic relationship that belongs to life as such. This tension is to be briefly sketched (1), and typical strategies of avoiding it are to be analyzed (2).

1. THE TENSION IN FREEDOM BETWEEN FINITY AND INFINITY

233. Freedom of the will is infinite in itself. Due to this freedom we are not confined to the ends and by the limits of a certain form like nonliving things, plants, and animals are. Due to this freedom we stand within an internally limitless horizon of goods in the world. Still, it is exactly this infinity that points us toward an experience of the finite that is not possible in such sharp focus for any "merely" finite being. Three levels of the tension arising between finity and infinity can be distinguished:

(1) Intrinsically infinite freedom is bound in its expression

by a many-layered past history. In order for a being, free in itself, to be able to achieve an effective capacity for free decisions, innumerable processes must have been successfully completed—beginning with the genesis of the Milky Way galaxy and our planetary system, beyond the processes of phylo- and ontogenetics, up to the developmental psychologistic and other thematizable events. The same configuration of processes that have led to the emergence of my freedom is, however, also responsible for my being confronted with this situation of decision with these and not any other alternatives. If one abstracts from earlier decisions, it is true: the alternatives of freedom are not a product of freedom.

(2) The transcendence beyond the determinate goods that are given along with freedom is in a sense lifted by an effectively free decision. For I bind myself in a free decision to a certain good that excludes all others and make myself finite in a specific way.

(3) A free being has the power of determining what it will be. This power does not cover freedom itself, however (and is naturally not limitless otherwise as regards content). For in every free positing the subject of freedom must assume itself as already posited, and not merely in objectifiable peculiarity, but also, and especially, as regards freedom itself to whose essential structure belongs its internal measure, the good extracted from the arbitrariness of factual desire. That is the form of finitude that is most internal to the infinite freedom.

234. This threefold tension between finity and infinity belongs to the structure of human freedom in all its situations. Because this tension structures the situation of free decisions, it is not an objectively establishable fact for the agent, but rather something to which he is related. How is that possible? The choice of deciding for oneself and not letting oneself be determined by other (heteronomous) factors lies in a sense prior to every free decision. This basic or "primitive" decision is naturally not a decision that could

stand on its own. It is rather an element of the concrete decisions that lies prior to them and is sometimes even conscious in the subject. This is especially the case if one attempts to tear oneself from a certain lifestyle in which one, in at least one or more realms, had let oneself go along with life more than one had determined one's own life. Thus, this basic decision, irrespective of its reference to concrete, individual decisions, has a greater generality than these individual decisions. Thus, it is natural that a content-filled correlate of greater generality corresponds to it: one manages to take one's life in hand, and this decision remains, not in a purely formal realm, but rather concretizes itself in a certain life project in which the concern is not this or that possible course of action but rather the whole course of life, that is, me as a whole person.

If a human being achieves a level of maturity in which she is capable of human freedom, then she will be confronted with situations in which she will be approached in the primitiveness and entirety of her self-accessibility. Whoever chooses positively for one or the other of the given possibilities thus ratifies the decision situation as the source of affirmable options. Whoever finds something in principle completely unbearable and unacceptable in the decision situation will deny the decision between the given alternatives as a whole. However, every decision situation might have something problematic in it due to the threefold tension sketched above. On the one hand, the decision situation must be accepted unconditionally so that it can be made into a free choice, but, on the other hand, it seems to demand the consent to a kind of dividedness. The problematic element is not always conscious for us, but there are situations in which we desperately search for further and other alternatives—in which we want to have simultaneously what is exclusive—in which we want to escape the having-to-decide on which the weight of the norms and responsibility depends. Thus, freedom becomes a large problem and not at all merely theoretical.

2. ATTEMPTS TO DISSOLVE THE TENSION IN FAVOR OF ONE SIDE

235. Here the search begins for possibilities of dissolving the problem—a search in whose course the subject becomes chafed and, due to this, perhaps wise. In what follows, the standpoint of the wise is taken over, who, looking back at her mistakes, discovers and interprets certain strategies of flight from something unavoidable. From the acknowledged false paths results perhaps a hint toward the true attitude. (One should not forget that it is easy to recognize false attitudes in others or in the abstract—but difficult to analyze one's own situation so that one realizes how one is doing.)

If one objectifies both poles of the tension, one can metaphorically remark that the human being stands in between an animal (or a lower being) and a god (a pure spirit). Animal and god seem to be closed, "rounded out" beings without the essential restlessness and eccentricity of the human being. For both are what they are, *complete:* existence without freedom or existence due to freedom. Thus, it can happen that human beings wish to be an animal or a god or act out of the secret hope of acting similar to a god or animal. Occasionally one assures oneself supportively through a theory that states that the human being is in principle either a fallen god or an alienated animal.

a) Denial of Finity

236. One way out of the problematic situation of freedom that is suggested first is an "idealistic" one—the path in which a subject identifies itself with its consciousness against its finity.

This denial of one's own finity stands behind attitudes like the following: the universal critic only allows for what is complete in every respect (and thus loses everything that he could live and love, up to an increase in the hate of everything that is not worth being there because it is faulty). The beautiful soul is reflected in its potentialities and is afraid of their disposal in order not to lose any of them (and thus disappears without formation). The rationalist cannot assume anything that she has not seen in a reconstructable manner (and decays out of pure distrust of gullibility regarding the next best hypothesis), and so on. The experience that one has during the attempt at denying one's finity is always twofold: on the one hand, it does not succeed, and, on the other hand, the (relative) success of the project does not lead to an emancipation of the spirit from its chains but rather leads to the loss of its fullness of reality. The fulfillment of the spirit and its redemption cannot directly be steered for. What is to be overcome—the power of background, of animality, of chance—is overpowered through this, in negative dialectic. "Whoever acts the angel becomes the beast" (Pascal, *Pensées* No. 358).

b) Denial of Infinity

237. After disappointment with the idealistic life project one can easily slide into its correlative opposite—into the negation of the idealistic negation that, as one must experience, still does not provide any positiveness.

Such a tendency is to be discovered behind the following attitude: one attempts to discard all questions about correctness and to live only according to spontaneous feeling (and must experience that spontaneity, made into a program, evinces tenseness as a consequence). One avoids one's responsibility by being led by what "one" (at that time) thinks and does (and must discover that one is also responsible for the consciously chosen conformity). One flees in sleep, depression, or intoxication (and awakens even more disappointed), and so on. The experience one has here is that for us no path takes us back to spontaneous and innocent animality if we have already entered into the mentally determined mode of existence. There exists an essential difference between the in a sense premental animality out of whose sphere the life of the mind arises (and *naturally* sinks back into periodically: sleep, automatic behavior, etc.) and the "project" animality, which is in its form mental and, therefore, internally incoherent. (In a similar vein this is true, as we tried to show, for the biological theories.)

The pole of the tension, *against* which one attempts to win one's wholeness, prevails destructively. In fact, one must in any project, unwillingly and — as one hopes — only initially, go through with (execute) the loathed or even denied dimension of freedom in order to be able to act at all. In this manner the impression grows that human existence is not capable of a unity but rather is absurdly constructed, without a solution.

II. Life from the Basic Tension

238. The impression that existence is internally absurd has a spiritualistic self-interpretation (and/or its counterpart, practical vitalism) as an indubitable basis. However, through the discouraging experiences with the spiritualistic theory and praxis the insight could mature that the correct path lies, not in flight from what we inevitably have to be, but rather in the acceptance of this existence. This acceptance cannot be a resigned laying down of one's weapons, for it is supposed to form the ground for an active engagement with life. It also cannot be a Yes with conditions, for the issue is to accept the uniquely real conditions—without my positing as conditions the fulfillment of certain desired changes or the successful justification of existence for the judgment of my reason. Still, this Yes demands more life and mental strength than the spiritualistic forms of Yes-But or No, not even mentioning the artificial Yes-forms of the vitalistic attitude.

It is strange, however, that we have to be *once more* what we *already* are, that is, that the basic act of freedom must be a repetition of what we already are. "A curious, indeed unearthly thing that we must first leap onto the soil on which we really stand" (M. Heidegger, *What Is Called Thinking?* New York 1968, 41).

Under what conditions is such an acceptance of oneself possible? (1) Is it worth the effort if everything sinks into nothingness in death? (2)

1. CONDITIONS FOR THE ACCEPTANCE
OF ONESELF

239. We ask about the objective, reality-grounded conditions under which the acceptance of one's own being is possible, disregarding the arbitrary "conditions" someone would perhaps like to dictate. Life is not a business partnership. What is to be accepted foremost is the finite, far too finite, element in our individual and common existence.

The realities which constitute and the laws which govern our lives can become the subject of knowledge, up to a certain degree. Such is the case when a general knowledge of human phenomena is gained and then applied to my concrete life. By knowing these determinations I stand in a distanced relationship to them. They are something in me, an it—not myself. If they were originally something that came to me from the outside, then they could not qualify the situation of the free subject from within. Therein they play a subordinate role, whether the concern is the historically produced states, properties of the human character, or necessary structures of the human condition. In any case they are nonarbitrary givens that belong to me as I stand here and now in a particular situation of action. From this it follows that their acceptance cannot occur in the same manner in which we come to terms with facts or attempts to make the best out of a situation when forced into it by external factors. Because the questionable determinations, despite all objectification and theoretical distance, are still mine, they are nothing else other than I am, a being determined in such and such a manner.

The acceptance of my limits is, thus, the acceptance of myself, that is, the acceptance of a person. This self-acceptance has the lawlike consequence of accepting another so that this other can be myself. As regard my tangible determinations I have received them just as contingently as another human being can enter my life. Of course, I have been assigned to myself since my birth without being conjoined with myself into a solid unity, so that the question could not arise anymore as to why I have to be the one that I am and not any other. However, as the human being which I have become can only develop—and thus indirectly enrich me—when I leave him room for his self-existence, it is also true for myself, the subject in its finite determinacy, in the eyes of the freely accepting and rejecting ego. Whoever is related to his own finity like the technician to his material or the master to his slave must experience that this personal material and this free slave cannot be tamed but rather gain dominance for themselves. One's self-relation is to have the influence of the attitude of a human being to her friend more than of the attitude of a technician to his things. (See also what was said about the body as a machine, No. 140, with the way of talking about the body as the "brother jackass" [Francis of Assisi].)

240. Since self-acceptance is a kind of interpersonal event, it stands in close connection with the acceptance of the human beings with whom I must associate. It does not belong to this acceptance that I say that everything about the other is good or that I submit my actions to the other's expectations—as little as it belongs to self-acceptance that I give my life free reign or that I claim to be a saint. Both modes (or dimensions) of this acceptance refer to an existence that lies deeper than the empirical properties that someone has or than the ways in which someone acts—rather they refer to being a person. This *needs* acceptance in order to develop properly. It comes to itself only in interpersonal and intrapersonal relationships to personal existence: precisely because it is essentially reliant upon the correct relation, it commands the whole moral order under which all actions stand (see No. 236). In normal experience it is the case that no one can really accept the human being who cannot accept himself (to at least a large extent). One must struggle very hard in order to accept oneself if one did not experience being accepted as a child. However, it is also the case that a part of accepting oneself occurs in the attempted acceptance of an-

other. At any rate the one cannot succeed against the other: the self-acceptance and affirmation that is connected with the denial of the right to exist for others and the charity that is motivated by flight from oneself.

However, how can I unconditionally accept a person in all his limitations? The moral demand to do so does not carry enough strength along with it. The strength can only grow to the extent that I become aware of the inner value of the person, relatively independent of his valuable or less valuable properties. This assumes that there is an order of goodness that comprehends an order of the various modes of competency (also moral) and acceptability. Due to the trust in the existence of goodness that is peculiar to every person, it is possible to accept someone who is bad or whom I do not immediately like. In this trust lies a certain amount of hope that the person in question is not limited to the present state of quality. In fact, human beings can develop beyond themselves when they experience that someone encounters them in this trusting and sanguine way. However, the correct ordering of motivation is decisive in good and bad. True acceptance does not determine but rather offers a new future, and the acceptance that is primarily achieved under the condition of a better future is fruitless because the real human being as she is is not being accepted but rather the human being as she should be.

2. THE PROBLEM OF DEATH

241. What hinders us from admitting the limited possibilities of our existence and from realizing ourselves in a finite way is a deeper consciousness of the solemnness of death for all finite beings. The more individuated a being is, the more possible points of attack it offers for destruction. Thus, the consciousness of the threat of death that is peculiar to human beings is immediately given along with his individual self-consciousness; the more the latter is developed, the

more the former is as well—at least in principle, thus setting aside the fact that the consciousness of mortality can hardly be borne without repression.

According to how I stand toward my existence, I will also stand toward death. If I suffer greatly in my existence—that I am such and not otherwise—I can view the dissolution of the limitations of my ego as desirable—even more desirable being that I would never have been born. The more I experience my life as meaningful, the more I will sense death as the fundamental threat. In both cases I imagine that death is an event in which something is taken from me: life that—seen in its essentials—is experienced in the one case as a burden, in the other as a gift. I myself, as the subject of life, remain behind: either freed from the limitations of individuality, somehow at one with the universe—or robbed of all possibilities of existence, absolutely naked.

242. If death is the dissolution of the ego's limitations in which the individuating movement is taken back, then, along with the limitations, the ego is lifted. If death takes away all powers of the subject, then the subject as such is neutralized. This is how it seems, and this impression is apparently confirmed by our knowledge of death that can be gained in an objective scientific way. Here death reveals itself as the destruction of the physiological foundation of individual life in all its levels, so that one must simply say: Peter who lived two days ago, that is, who counted as a real being, has stopped existing. The argument that I am incapable of *imagining* my death other than a change of state does not arise against the harshness of this judgment: the psychological grammatical permanence of the ego that imagines itself dead is uncovered by objective observation as something merely subjective. The inconceivable simple nonexistence swallows us up, and when all human beings who might remember us or whose conditions of existence were created by us are dead, then it will be as if we had never existed.

One can attempt to evade this fact either by repressing any

consciousness thereof that may arise (which appears to be naturally implanted in us) or by pointing out that one continues to live on in whatever one has identified with and endures longer than us: in one's offspring and works, one's social institution or class. However, neither the one nor the other can succeed. Regarding repression that is clear anyway. It is also easy to see for identification. For, on the one hand, my varying identifications do not exhaust the totality of my identity. Whoever attempts to live like this has a very disturbed (fanatical, etc.) self-makeup. On the other hand, all of my identifications ultimately take the same path as I do, the path into nonexistence. A more delicate way of evading the fact lies in pointing out the necessary function of dying among beings that reproduce sexually and in emphasizing the positive role of death for the significance of particular life situations and life in its entirety, as it is not repeatable. Both lines of thought hit on something correct. The second, by the way, is an argument against the possibility of starting over again from the beginning as is implied in the teaching of reincarnation. However, as much as we have the insight that it is unreasonable to wish that life would just continue on forever, this insight does not console us with the idea of the absolute nonexistence (or not-any-more-existence).

243. If nonexistence can attack us at any moment and simply wipe us out, what weight can our present existence have — and have in all truth — beyond the feeling of importance that comes from the childish egocentric conception of ourselves and that consists, for the most part, in illusions? If we attempt not to pretend at all, what reason remains as to why we should engage ourselves in and with life? Probably none at all, for the continuation of life — as much natural wisdom as might be contained in it! — cannot constitute a valid reason in itself for a thinking human being.

Such a reason for continuation can only consist in the fact that whatever we bring forth in the purest acts of freedom — and that is foremost freed personal existence — somehow remains intact after death. It is only when this is the case that life is worthwhile for a thinking human being—not as if earthly existence justified itself through a "later," "other-worldly" existence such that without this remaining intact and being saved, earthly existence would prove to be directionless and weightless. However, *can* it be such in light of the radicality of decline in death? The radicality of the loss of power of the subject in death is not the question here. However, is the objective statement that the subject simply ceases to exist in death justified? One can point out that no thinking, choosing, or sensing is possible without a functioning brain. Since, however, (see No. 165ff. and No. 192) this connection is only of an empirical nature and cannot be insightful as an essential connection, the possibility is not to be excluded that the personal carrier of mental thought and wanting needs a healthy human body for its earthly mode of existence and manifestation, but not to its existence *per se*. This nonimpossibility suffices in order to justify the "noble risk" (Plato, *Phaedo* 114 d) toward which freedom pushes in its internal dynamics: to live as if death had no power over our actual existence. For both of the other practical alternatives to it are either immediate suicide or the renunciation of a determined life of freedom, obligated to the intrinsically truthful and valuable.

III. Philosophical Anthropology and Theology

244. The relation that relates itself to itself posits itself—not simply but rather as a relation that has already assumed itself. With this feature it necessarily develops an idea of what has posited it and a position next to that being posited, although this must not occur to any extent consciously. "The self of human beings is a relation that is related to itself and by being related to itself is related to another . . . that has posited the whole relation" (Kierkegaard, *Sickness unto Death,* IAa).

The relation which constitutes our being is itself constituted. One might be inclined to interpret this reality simply as the fact that we are the product of highly complex natural processes, as do the various types of materialism. However, as soon as one reflects that here a free self-relation is being brought forth, the natural reduction drops to the level of a merely partial explanation that cannot get the decisive point—the self-givenness—into its view. The human being who thinks the origin (and future) of his existence materialistically is not thinking on the level on which he, as a thinking being, lives (which remains true even if he should live as a "practical materialist").

However, how are we to interpret our origin otherwise? Everything seems obscure here. Perhaps we will come closer to the reason why we are free and thinking beings if we consider in what the ground for particular conceivable thoughts and particular affirmable values lies. Why do theoretical problems arise for us when their solutions have no practical relevance for our lives? From where does it come that we can solve such problems—at least negatively through the exclusion of false answers? From where does it come that a moral obligation can arise for us in a certain situation—that a human being, a landscape, or a piece of music can be so beautiful that we are torn into an ineffable condition? In such experiences of truth, good, and beauty we feel that we become more of a human being and comprehend what is happening here much less than the functional-mechanical interpretable processes of our physique and psyche. Such experiences do not occur very often, but to a small degree we have them constantly, hardly paying attention anymore; and that points toward the fact that the sphere out of which the extraordinary experiences come define in principle the sphere of our human life. Ultimately, and in the decisive point, wanting to comprehend hits upon a "cloud of unknowable things"—not due to an external limit of our epistemic apparatus but rather because the concern is the origin and the possibility of knowledge, of affirming and being able to choose, of being beautiful and being able to be fascinated which encompasses everything, substantial existence and particular act-events alike, as an origin.

245. That this origin cannot be a material process is already evident. However, it cannot be an emanation of the intrinsic, pure ideal truth, good, and beauty into the material either, separate at first and then mediated through a subject that would be pure passage. The origin at which we are aiming must leave behind the difference in it between ideality and reality because this difference emerges from it. This original secret that can only be represented for objective consciousness by pictures and analogies is named by the religious human being with the exceedingly old and ambiguous name "God."

The divine origin is in everything that we can encounter and just as immanent as transcendent. It is immanent insofar as all existence, cognitive accessibility, goodness, and so on, all knowledge and love participate in its existence, light, affirmation, and life — and transcendent at the same time insofar as true independence from the nondivine is justified and grows through this participation, up to the free availability over oneself, in one's finite infinite structure. In this personal finite infinite act — not only in the infinite component thereof — the divine origin is "there": more internal to us than we can be ourselves (Augustine, *Confessions* III,6,11).

246. The peculiarity of the living organism "human being" and thus the irreducibility of all anthropological sciences to physics (in the widest sense, the descriptive and explanatory natural sciences) depend on this ontologically basic relation of our existence to God. Ultimately all forms of humanitarian ethics depend on it as well. Thus, the proclamation of the "death of man" (M. Foucault) is only the consequent completion of the announcement of "God's death" (Nietzsche) if the latter it taken radically (see Derrida 1976). Presumably one must go one step further. As a comparison of the history of human ideas with the essentialistic dualistic anthropologies of the Greek classical period shows, the thought that the spiritual-bodily, individual human being has an irreducible existence and a true unity has become a general conviction in the background of the specifically Christian belief in God as the being that is immanent and transcendent for his creation and "becoming" man himself. In this sense the modern attempts at philosophical anthropology have, in one way or another, a concealed relation to Christology.

Bibliography

Adorno, Theodor W., *et alii, Der Positivismusstreit in der deutschen Soziologie,* Darmstadt-Neuwied 1987

Baumgartner, Hans-Michael, "Über die Widerspenstigheit der Vernunft, sich aus Geschichte erklären zu lassen: Zur Kritik des Selbstverständnisses der evolutionären Erkenntnistheorie," in Poser, Hans (Hrsg.), *Wandel des Vernunftbegriffs,* Freiburg-München 1981, 39–64

Beck, Lewis White, *The Actor and the Spectator,* New Haven 1975

Beck, Lewis White, *A Commentary on Kant's Critique of Practical Reason,* Chicago 1960

Blondel, Maurice, *Action,* translated by Oliva Blanchette, Notre Dame 1984

Boss, Medard, *Grundriss der Medizin,* Bern 1971

Breuer, Reinhard, *Das anthropische Prinzip: Der Mensch im Fadenkreuz der Naturgesetze,* München 1983

Bruaire, Claude, *Philosophie du corps,* Paris 1968

Büchel, Wolfgang, *Philosophische Probleme der Physik,* Freiburg 1965

Bühler, Karl, *Sprachtheorie: Die Darstellungs-Funktion der Sprache,* Jena 1934

Buytendijk, F. J. J., *Mensch und Tier: Ein Beitrag zur vergleichenden Psychologie,* Hamburg-Reinbek 1958

Carnois, Bernard, *La cohérence de la doctrine kantienne de la liberté,* Paris 1973

Carr, Edward, *What Is History?* New York 1962

Derrida, Jacques, "Fines hominis," in J. D., *Randgänge der Philosophie,* Berlin 1976, 88–123. (*Marges de la philosophie,* Paris 1972, 129–164)

Derrida, Jacques, *Of Grammatology,* Baltimore 1976

193

Eccles, John Carew, *The Human Psyche.* The Gifford Lectures. University of Edinburgh 1978–1979, Berlin-Heidelberg 1980

Eccles, John Carew, *The Neurophysiological Basis of Mind: The Principles of Neurophysiology,* Oxford 1953

Eccles, John Carew, *The Wonder of Being Human,* New York 1984

Eibl-Eibesfeldt, Irenäus, "Stammesgeschichtliche Anpassungen im Verhalten des Menschen," in Gadamer-Vogler II (1972), 3–59

Eliade, Mircea, *Kosmos und Geschichte,* Hamburg-Reinbek 1966. (*Cosmos and History: The Myth of the Eternal Return,* New York 1959)

Erikson, Erik H., *Childhood and Society,* New York 1963

Erikson, Erik H., "Das Problem der Identität," in *Psyche* 10 (1956/57) 114–176

Fast, Julius, *Body Language,* New York 1970

Freud, Sigmund, *The Complete Introductory Lectures on Psychoanalysis,* New York 1966

Frey, Gerhard, "Möglichkeit und Bedeutung einer evolutionären Erkenntnistheorie," in *Zeitschrift für philosophische Forschung* 34 (1980) 1–17

Gadamer, Hans-Georg, *Truth and Method,* New York 1975

Gadamer, Hans-Georg, and Vogler, Paul, *Neue Anthropologie,* 7 vols., Stuttgart-München 1972/75

Gehlen, Arnold, *Anthropologische Forschung: Zur Selbstbegegnung und Selbstentdeckung des Menschen,* Hamburg-Reinbek 1961

Gehlen, Arnold, *Man, His Nature and Place in the World,* New York 1988

Gipper, Helmut, "Der Beitrag der inhaltlich orientierten Sprachwissenschaft zur Kritik der historischen Vernunft," in H. G., *Denken ohne Sprache?* Dusseldorf 1971, 56–80

Gipper, Helmut, *Das Sprachapriori: Sprache als Voraussetzung menschlichen Denkens und Erkennens,* Stuttgart 1987

Grom, Bernhard, "Rehabilitation des Geistes? Die Wiederentdeckung des Kognitiven und Subjektiven in der neueren Verhaltenspsychologie," in *Stimmen der Zeit* 200 (1982) 89–103

Haeffner, Gerd, "Ontologische Randnotizen zum Sinn der Frage 'Was ist der Mensch?'" in *Zeitschrift für katholische Theologie* 102 (1980) 217–225

Hassenstein, B., "Das spezifisch Menschliche nach den Resultaten der Verhaltensforschung," in Gadamer-Vogler II (1972) 60–97

Hegel, Georg Wilhelm Friedrich, *Vorlesungen über die Philosophie der Geschichte* (Werke in 20 Bänden, Bd. 12), Frankfurt 1970. (*Lectures on the Philosophy of World History,* Cambridge 1975)

Heidegger, Martin, *The Basic Problems of Phenomenology,* Bloomington 1982

Heidegger, Martin, *Being and Time,* New York 1962

Heidegger, Martin, *Identity and Difference,* New York 1969

Heidegger, Martin, "On the Essence of Truth," in *Basic Writings,* New York 1977, 117–141

Heidegger, Martin, *On the Way to Language,* New York 1971

Heidegger, Martin, *What Is Called Thinking?* New York 1968

Heisenberg, Werner, *Physics and Philosophy,* New York 1962

Homann, K., "Geschichtslosigkeit," in *Historisches Wörterbuch der Philosophie,* hrsg. v. J. Ritter, Bd. 3, Basel 1974, Sp. 413–416

Humboldt, Wilhelm von, *Über die Verschiedenheit des menschlichen Sprachbaues und ihren Einfluss auf die geistige Entwicklung des Menschengeschlechts,* Berlin 1830/35. (Werke, Akademie-Ausgabe, Bd. VII)

Husserl, Edmund, *Ideas: General Introduction to Pure Phenomenology,* New York 1962

Jacobi, Jolande, *The Way of Individuation,* New York 1967

Jacobi, Jolande, *The Psychology of C.G. Jung,* London 1968

Keller, Albert, *Sprachphilosophie,* Freiburg-München 1979

Kierkegaard, Sören, *Sickness Unto Death,* Princeton 1941

Koselleck, Reinhart, *Futures Past: On the Semantics of Historical Time,* Cambridge 1985

Levinas, Emmanuel, *Totality and Infinity,* Pittsburgh 1969

Lévi-Strauss, Claude, "Culture et nature: La condition humaine à la lumière de l'anthropologie," in *Commentaire* 4 (Paris 1981) 365–372

Lévi-Strauss, Claude, *Der nackte Mensch* (Mythologica, IV), Frankfurt 1975. (*The Naked Man,* New York 1981)

Lorenz, Konrad, "Die angeborenen Formen möglicher Erfahrung," in *Zeitschrift für Tierpsychologie* 5 (1943) 235–409

Lorenz, Konrad, *Behind the Mirror,* New York 1977

Lorenz, Konrad, *The Foundations of Ethology,* New York 1981

Lotz, Johannes B., *Der Mensch im Sein,* Freiburg 1967

Marcel, Gabriel, *Being and Having,* New York 1965

Martinet, André, *Elements of General Linguistics,* Chicago 1964

Matthes, Joachim, "Soziologie: Schlüsselwissenschaft des 20. Jahrhunderts," in Matthes, J. (Hrsg.), *Lebenswelt und soziale Probleme: Verhandlungen des 20. Deutschen Soziologentages zu Bremen 1980,* Frankfurt 1982, 15–27

Merleau-Ponty, Maurice, *Phenomenology of Perception,* New York 1962

Müller, Max, *Erfahrung und Geschichte: Grundzüge einer Philosophie der Freiheit als transzendentale Erfahrung,* Freiburg-München 1971

Müller, Max, *Philosophische Anthropologie,* Hrsg. von Wilhelm Vossenkuhl, mit einem Beitrag "Zur gegenwartigen Anthropologie," Freiburg-München 1974

Müller, Max, *Sinn-Deutungen der Geschichte,* Zürich 1976

Müller, Max, and Halder, Alois (Hrsg.), *Kleines philosophisches Wörterbuch,* Freiburg 1971

Pannenberg, Wolfhart, *Anthropology in Theological Perspective,* Philadelphia 1985

Pascal, Blaise, *Thoughts on Religion,* Oxford and London 1851

Peursen, Cornelis A. van, *Body, Soul, Spirit,* London and Oxford 1966

Plessner, Helmut, *Philosophische Anthropologie,* Frankfurt 1970

Plessner, Helmut, *Die Stufen des Organischen und der Mensch,* Berlin 1928

Portmann, Adolf, *Die Biologie und das neue Menschenbild,* Bern 1942

Portmann, Adolf, *An den Grenzen des Wissens,* Düsseldorf 1974

Portmann, Adolf, *Zoologie und das neue Bild des Menschen,* Hamburg-Reinbek 1956

Pothast, Ulrich (Hrsg.), *Seminar: Freis Handeln und Determinismus,* Frankfurt 1978

Pothast, Ulrich, *Die Unzulänglichkeit der Freiheitsbeweise: Zu einigen Lehrstücken aus der neueren Geschichte von Philosophie und Recht,* Frankfurt 1980

Rahner, Karl, *Foundations of Christian Faith,* New York 1978

Ricken, Friedo, "Zur Freiheitsdiskussion in der sprachanalytischen Philosophie," in *Theologie und Philosophie* 52 (1977) 525–542

Rickert, Heinrich, *System der Philosophie* I. Teil: Allgemeine Grundlegung der Philosophie, Tübingen 1921

Riedl, Rupert, *Biology of Knowledge: The Evolutionary Basis of Reason,* New York 1984

Sartre, Jean-Paul, *Being and Nothingness,* New York 1956

Saussure, Ferdinand de, *Course in General Linguistics,* New York 1959

Scheler, Max, *Formalism in Ethics and Non-Formal Ethics of Values,* Evanston 1973

Scheler, Max, *Man's Place in Nature,* Boston 1961

Scheler, Max, *Zur Phänomenologie und Metaphysik der Freiheit (1912 bis 1914),* in Gesammelte Werke, Bd. 10, Bern 1957, 155–178

Schelsky, Helmut, *Die Arbeit tun die anderen: Klassenkampf und Priesterherrschaft der Intellektuellen,* Opladen 1975

Schilder, Paul, *Das Körperschema,* Berlin 1923

Schulz, Walter, *Philosophie in der veränderten Welt,* Pfullingen 1972

Schwidetzky, Ilse, "Variationsstatistische Untersuchungen über Anthropologie-Definitionen," in *Homo* 25 (1975) 1–10, 37f.

Spitz, René A., *First Year of Life,* New York 1965

Spitz, René A., *Vom Säugling zum Kleinkind,* Stuttgart 1967

Straus, Erwin, "Über Anosognosie," in *Jahrbuch für Psychologie und Psychotherapie* 11 (1964) 26–42

Straus, Erwin: *Vom Sinn der Sinne: Ein Beitrag zur Grundlegung der Psychologie,* Berlin-Göttingen-Heidelberg 1956

Theunissen, Michael, *The Other: Studies in the Social Ontology of Husserl, Heidegger, Sartre and Buber,* Cambridge, MA 1984

Theunissen, Michael, "Skeptische Betrachtungen über den anthropologischen Personbegriff," in H. Rombach (Hrsg.), *Die Frage nach dem Menschen,* München-Freiburg 1966, 461–490

Tinland, Frank, *La différence anthropologique: Essai sur les rapports de la nature et de l'artifice,* Paris 1977

Tugendhat, Ernst, *Self-Consciousness and Self-Determination,* Cambridge, MA 1986

Uexküll, Jakob von, *Streifzuge durch die Umwelten von Tieren und Menschen,* Hamburg-Reinbek 1956

Vogel, Gunter, and Angermann, Hartmut, *dtv-Atlas zur Biologie,* 2 Bde., München, 15. Aufl. 1980

Vollmer, Gerhard, *Evolutionäre Erkenntnistheorie: Angeborene Erkenntnisstrukturen im Kontext von Biologie, Psychologie,*

Linguistik, Philosophie und Wissenschaftstheorie, Stuttgart 1975

Vollmer, Gerhard, *Was können wir wissen? Vol. I.: Die Natur der Erkenntnis: Beiträge zur evolutionären Erkenntnistheorie,* Stuttgart 1985

Whorf, Benjamin, *Language, Thought and Reality,* London 1956

Wickler, Wolfgang, and Seibt, Uta, *Das Prinzip Eigennutz: Ursachen und Konsequenzen sozialen Verhaltens,* Hamburg 1977

Wilson, Edward O., *Biologie als Schicksal: Die soziobiologischen Grundlagen menschlichen Verhaltens,* Frankfurt-Berlin-Wien 1980. (*On Human Nature,* Harvard 1978)

Wilson, Edward O., *Sociobiology: The New Synthesis,* Cambridge, MA 1975

Zaner, Richard M., *The Problem of Embodiment: Some Contributions to a Phenomenology of the Body,* Den Haag 1964

Index